FORGED: 52 Weeks of Grit, Growth, and Grace for Men Who Don't Like to Read

Published by Sonfire Media, LLC
Galax, VA 24333 USA

ISBN No. 978-0-9845515-7-6

FORGED

52 Weeks of Grit, Growth, and Grace
for Men Who Don't Like to Read

SONFIRE MEDIA
A PUBLISHING COMPANY

sonfiremedia.com
GALAX, VA

LARRY W. VANHOOSE

Dedication

I dedicate this book to my best friend—
the Master Smith, the Maker of our souls, the one true
Creator who patiently shapes each of us, who are willing,
into "a vessel unto honour, sanctified, and meet for the
master's use, and prepared unto every good work."
2 Timothy 2:21b KJV

Hebrews 12:29 KJV

"For our God is a consuming fire."

Table of Contents

Acknowledgments	IX
Foreword	X
Read This First	XIII
Stage One – Foundation & Identity	1
Week 1: A Chance to Breathe	3
Week 2: A Father's Love	7
Week 3: Under an Open Sky	11
Week 4: Be Still	13
Week 5: On the Edge	19
Week 6: Weeds	23
Week 7: True Valentine	27
Week 8: Ancient of Days	31
Stage Two – Wrestling & Awakening	35
Week 9: Horse Sense	37
Week 10: 5 + 2 = 5000 (With 12 Left Over)	41
Week 11: Hope Springs Eternal	45
Week 12: A Legacy of Love	49
Week 13: Don't Lose Your Head	53
Week 14: Mr. Doesn't Matter	57
Week 15: Roots	61
Week 16: Beloved	65
Stage Three – Surrender & Freedom	69
Week 17: Soul Food	71
Week 18: Lock and Key	75
Week 19: Surrounded	79
Week 20: You Will Surely Die	83
Week 21: Off Track	87
Week 22: Breathing Lessons	91
Week 23: The Sacred Paradigm Shift	95
Week 24: What For?	99
Stage Four – Perseverance Under Pressure	103

Table of Contents (cont'd.)

Week 25: Seven Long Days   105

Week 26: Where Is God?   109

Week 27: Words to Live By   111

Week 28: This is Not a Spectator Sport   115

Week 29: God and Power Tools   117

Week 30: You're Not Finished   121

Week 31: God Doesn't Waste Dirt   125

Week 32: Field of Dreams   127

Stage Five – Perseverance Under Pressure   131

Week 33: A Dollar an Hour   133

Week 34: Arms Wide Open   135

Week 35: Faith Floats   137

Week 36: Mustard Seed TV   139

Week 37: MTV   143

Week 38: Screwed Up   147

Week 39: Whoa, Nellie!   151

Week 40: That's Not My Thought   155

Week 41: Pride Rock   159

Week 42: In Living Color   163

Week 43: The Greatest Mystery   167

Week 44: The Real World   171

Stage Six – Love & Legacy   175

Week 45: River of Life   177

Week 46: Tony the Tiger   181

Week 47: Kilroy Was Here   185

Week 48: No Greater Love   189

Week 49: Choose Your Family   193

Week 50: The Pink Pig   197

Week 51: The Little Drummer Boy   201

Week 52: The Shepherd's Staff   203

Last Call – The Line in the Sand   207

Acknowledgments

My heartfelt gratitude to my wife, Trina, for her patient and loving support during the years it took to pull this project together; to my wonderful children for their inspiration and grace towards me as I try to "larn' it as I live it"; to my dear friend, partner, and mentor William "Sam" Bartlett, who is always there to listen and advise when asked; and finally to my editor and great friend, Vie Stallings Herlocker, for her tireless investment in this work, and her dogged determination to see it finally in print.

You all are the best!

Foreword

As a bodybuilder and horse trainer who also operates a fitness center, I like to think of myself as a hip upper-middle-aged man. I subscribe to multiple podcasts on longevity and have curated an elite collection of anti-aging supplements. I play tennis and basketball with men half my age and work long hours managing multiple other businesses, from real estate to restaurants. Oh, I also invest substantial resources walking alongside men who have lost it all due to addiction and who are seeking to heal and rebuild. This is how I "think" of myself and how I am perceived by most others in my small community. Sam Bartlett - a community leader, family man, and a spiritual guide to many.

And then there is the real me:

The subtle reminders that at the age of sixty-six, there are more years behind me than in front of me, regardless of my healthy lifestyle. What is my true purpose? Why am I chasing my tail with so many activities?

The self-awareness of my sins and failures. Would people still love me if they knew all that I have thought and done?

The buried pain from the recent death of a son. What the hell, God?

The loneliness of maxing out my friends list on Facebook, and yet struggling to identify true connections. Are there other men out there who have a hard time separating what is real from what is fake?

The onetime pastor and spiritual leader who now has as many questions as answers. How can I reconnect to the joy of my salvation?

The sad truth is I got very comfortable in my semi-miserable spiritual state. As long as I kept moving, I could drown out the yearnings for a deeper walk with God. I could keep pretending that I did not need a spiritual reset, and it is easy to fool most people around you who are too busy with their own struggles.

And then, Larry VanHoose asked me to read and review his new book, Forged: 52 Weeks of Grit, Growth, and Grace for Men Who Don't Like to Read. Of course I said yes, because as you have already learned, I can't say no. My expectations were low until I started reading. Just a few pages in, and I realized that God was speaking directly to me through these pages.

I could not stop reading, not only because the writing is clear, concise, and compelling, but because I no longer felt alone. Here was a man who was not afraid to share the grittiness of his own journey and how Jesus met him in the low moments, not just the high moments. In Larry's words, "the living Son of God who meets us right in the middle of the mess." I felt like Larry understood me and my struggles. I am still far from perfect, but this devotional has inspired me to strengthen my spirit, not just my body.

The book is not without flaws. Larry tricks us by saying it is for men who do not like to read and that you have up to 52 weeks to get through it (one chapter per week). Trust me, you will not be able to wait that long to get to the next chapter. I would have titled it 52 days. When you are thirsty and need a drink, it is hard to stop. If you want to stay spiritually hydrated, this book is for you.

— William "Sam" Bartlett, Jr.

✓ Read This First —
(Even If You Don't Like Reading)

If you're holding this book, chances are someone shoved it into your hands and said, "This is for you." Or maybe you surprised yourself and grabbed it anyway. Either way – respect. Let's be honest, most of us guys don't need more fluff. We need something real.

Here's the deal, life isn't meaningless. You were created with purpose. But if you can't tell the real from the fake, the authentic from the cheap knockoffs, you're going to get beat up by life more than necessary. That's why this book is called *Forged*. Because there are two kinds of forging. One is counterfeit – a forgery. Fake, hollow, and flimsy. The other comes through fire – metal heated, hammered, and shaped into something strong and true. Every man has to decide which kind of forging will define his life.

When I trained in martial arts, I often had to spar against my sensei. He was a multiple-discipline, third-degree black belt who always seemed to know my move before I made it. Painful? Absolutely. Humiliating? More than once. But every bruise, every mistake, every correction made me stronger, quicker, sharper. That's the fight of life. Hard, painful – but it shapes us if we don't quit.

These devotionals come out of my own battles, regrets, failures, and struggles I'd rather forget – the "grittiness" of my life. But here's what I've learned – God doesn't waste pain. He forges true grit in us through struggle, growth through reflection, and grace through Jesus. Not a myth, not a fairy tale – the living Son of God who meets us right in the middle of the mess.

So here's the challenge, don't skip out. Read one paragraph a day or knock out a chapter once a week. However you do it, keep showing up.

This isn't about reading – it's about becoming.

Becoming forged by fire – not a forgery – into His likeness (2 Corinthians 3:18).

Stage 1

Foundation & Identity

Week 1 —
A Chance to Breathe

The first time I sprained my knee, I shrugged it off. The second time, I got ticked. When I messed up the other knee, I had to admit it – my "keep running no matter what" plan wasn't going to work.

That was hard to swallow for a guy who used to run five, six, sometimes seven days a week. Long before I met my wife – and for years into our marriage – running was my thing. My stress relief. My competition. My "me time."

When people asked why I ran so much, I had a go-to answer, "There's an old fat guy chasing me, and I'm trying to keep him from catching up." I wasn't talking about somebody else. I was talking about me – the version I was afraid I'd become if I slowed down.

So I didn't slow down. I ran like the Energizer Bunny with a gym bag – mile after mile, day after day. But the knee injuries kept coming – right knee, left knee, back to the right again. Every time I thought I was ready to run, I'd be icing my leg before the week was over.

I still went to the gym, but it wasn't the same. I missed the pounding rhythm of my feet on the pavement. I missed that moment in the run when the noise in my head got quiet and everything clicked. And yeah, I could feel that "old fat guy" gaining on me.

Eventually, I stopped trying to run. My knees needed rest. My pride probably did too.

And that's when something surprising happened.

I started walking. Slowly. No stopwatch. No ear buds blasting music to keep me moving. Just me, my thoughts, and my dogs. We wandered through the woods on our farm, crossed meadows, followed the gravel road until it disappeared around a bend.

At first, I thought walking would be boring. But I started noticing things – birds darting across the trail, the bite of cool air in the morning, sunrises stretching pink and gold across the sky. Stuff I hadn't noticed in years.

It wasn't just my knees that needed healing. My soul did, too.

All those years, I thought the "win" was in the running. Push harder. Go faster. Outrun the guy I was afraid of becoming. But in all that motion, I was missing the stillness – the place where God meets you without a stopwatch or a finish line.

Walking slowed my legs, but more importantly, it slowed my mind. It reminded me that rest isn't losing – it's part of the plan. Even God Himself rested after six days of creation. If He could take a break, why did I think I didn't need one?

Now, I'm running again. But it's not the same. I'm not running *from* anything. I'm not trying to outrun the "old fat guy." I'm running *in* the moment. Eyes open. Breathing deep. Grateful for the gift of movement instead of obsessing over how fast or how far I go.

And if I get injured again? I know the way back – stillness, breath, grace.

God never asked us to live maxed out and worn down. He told us to run His race – with endurance, with purpose, and with our eyes on Him. Sometimes that means full stride. Sometimes it means slowing to a walk so He can catch up with your weary heart.

"…and let us run with endurance the race God has set before us. We do this by keeping our eyes on Jesus…" (Hebrews 12:1–2 NLT).

Growth
When's the last time you gave yourself permission to slow down – not because you had to, but because it was the wisest thing to do?

Grace
Sometimes the holiest thing you can do is stop, breathe, and let God catch up with you.

Week 2 —
A Father's Love

Somewhere on the six-hour drive back from visiting my dad, I glanced over at the passenger seat. My eighteen-year-old son was asleep – head against the window, mouth half open, breathing deep. I glanced up into the rearview mirror to see my daughter too asleep, snuggled into the corner of the backseat, legs tucked up into her arms and her head against the pillow she'd brought for that purpose.

And there it was again. That wave I've felt a thousand times before – pure, unfiltered, unapologetic love. The kind that can't be explained to someone who's never had a kid.

I don't mean "love" like you love a good steak or a winning touchdown. I mean the kind that hits you in the chest so hard it almost knocks the wind out of you. You'd take a bullet without thinking. You'd trade places in a hospital bed without hesitation. You'd give up anything – everything – for this kid.

And yet… there's one thing stronger.

God's love for us.

Paul puts it like this,

"I am convinced that neither death nor life, neither angels nor demons, neither the present nor the future, nor any powers... will be able to separate us from the love of God that is in Christ Jesus our Lord" (Romans 8:38–39).

Or this one,

"But God demonstrates his own love for us in this: While we were still sinners, Christ died for us" (Romans 5:8 NLT).

Let that sink in – before we got our act together, before we even wanted Him, God loved us enough to die for us.

I love my kids deeply. But I'll admit, sometimes they test my patience. We don't always see eye to eye. We don't always agree on... well, a lot of things. But here's the crazy part, every time I see them, my love grows. It's like a river pushing against a dam – it just builds until it spills over.

And that's me – a flawed, impatient, imperfect dad.

God's love isn't like that. It doesn't fade when we mess up. It doesn't thin out over time. It's constant. It's complete. It's stronger than the worst thing you've ever done and bigger than the best thing you'll ever do.

Jesus put it in simple, dad-language,

"Which of you, if his son asks for bread, will give him a stone? Or... a snake? If you, then, though you are evil, know how to give good gifts to your children – how much more will your Father in heaven give good gifts to those who ask him!" (Matthew 7:9–11)

That's God saying, "If you think *your* love for your kid is strong, you haven't seen anything yet."

So here's my advice – don't just read about His love. Ask Him to let you feel it. Really feel it. Not in a "that was a nice sermon" way, but in a "my knees are weak, and my chest might explode" kind of way.

If He can love you more than you love your own child, then knowing that – experiencing that – changes everything.

Because once you get it, you stop living like you're trying to earn it. You start living like you already have it.

"Ask and it will be given to you; seek and you will find; knock and the door will be opened to you" (Matthew 7:7).

Go ahead – ask Him. What could it hurt?

Growth

When was the last time you simply asked God to let you experience His love – not just know it in your head, but feel it in your bones?

Grace

You are deeply, eternally loved by your Father – and nothing can change that.

Week 3 — *Under an Open Sky*

When I was ten, my parents decided they'd had enough of cheap, questionable roadside motels on our annual family trips. We loved to travel, but the nicer hotels and inns were almost always out of our budget. That's why it was such a shock – and a thrill – when my sister and I came home from school one afternoon to find a small, used camper parked in our driveway.

I can still remember running my hands along the aluminum siding, peeking inside at the little dinette table, the fold-down beds, and the built-in storage. It felt like we'd just been handed the keys to a new world. At the time, we had no idea how much that one simple decision – buying a used camper – would change the rhythm of our lives.

We weren't a church-going family, so Sundays didn't look much different from Saturdays. Dad would tinker with cars in the garage while NASCAR hummed in the background. Mom worked on projects at home or picked up extra shifts at the hospital where she was a nurse. My sister and I rode bikes, played ball, or roamed the neighborhood with friends. Life in our small town was slow and predictable.

Then came camping. Once the headache of finding a decent motel was gone – and remember, there was no Google or online booking back then – we could travel whenever time and budget allowed. That first little camper eventually gave way to bigger ones, each upgrade bringing a little more comfort. By the time my sister and I were teenagers and Dad had started his own business, we were camping somewhere across North America a couple of weekends each month and for weeks at a time in the summer. Sometimes just us, sometimes with friends or relatives, but always with a sense of adventure.

It was in those travels that my world started to open up. Sleeping under a sky full of stars. Watching campfire embers glow deep red. Chasing crawdads in cold mountain streams. Climbing ridges with the wind in my face. Somewhere in those moments, I began to notice beauty I hadn't really seen before.

I didn't yet know God personally, but I could see the brush strokes of His handiwork everywhere I looked.

Camping taught me how to be still and how to notice. It showed me how the rhythm of nature – the rise and set of the sun, the gentle lapping of water against a riverbank, the chorus of crickets at night – can quiet the noise in your head. Even before I had a relationship with Him, God was planting seeds in my heart, using the wide-open spaces of His creation to whisper His presence.

Years later, I can still say the camping fever never left me. God used those trips to shake me awake from the small, self-focused bubble of my youth. Over time, He broke my self-centered heart and replaced it with a hunger to know His people – people from every culture, every background, every walk of life.

These days, I can sit for hours listening to a grandmother tell stories from her porch. I can watch the wonder in a child's eyes as they see a newborn fawn for the first time. I can stand on the shoreline and hear the waves crash while gulls swoop down for a fisherman's catch.

The stories of the road and the life lived outdoors never grow old to me. And the storytellers? They never really disappear. They just move on to another campsite. For me, that's what it's like to go camping – camping with God.

Jesus knew something about that kind of life. He often stepped away from the crowds to pray in quiet places. And in Matthew 8:20, He said,

"Foxes have dens to live in, and birds have nests, but the Son of Man has no place even to lay his head."

He knew the value of being outside the walls, meeting with the Father under an open sky.

Growth

When was the last time you truly stepped away from the noise and routine to be alone with God? How might you plan that kind of "camping trip" for your soul in the coming weeks?

Grace

The wide-open spaces of God's creation can awaken your heart to see Him more clearly.

Week 4 —
Be Still

Do you have trouble listening? I'm not talking about just hearing the sounds, but really listening – tuning in so you catch the meaning and not just the noise.

I do. And in my case, there's a medical reason. I was born without one of the components of the inner ear in my left ear – the cochlea. Everything else is there – the eardrum, the little bones in the middle ear, all the parts that should work together to get sound where it needs to go. But without the cochlea, the vibrations my outer ear picks up never get converted into electrical signals my brain can process.

In plain English: my left ear can hear, but my brain never gets the message.

That little detail about me explains something people have noticed since I was a kid, when you talk to me, I'll look you full in the face – especially if you're anywhere from straight ahead to my left side. I'm not being intense or overly serious. I'm just making sure I can actually understand you. I turn my good ear toward you and watch your lips. I can't "half listen" while doing something else. If I want to hear you, I have to focus.

One interesting thing from all those hearing tests when I was young

– I could feel the vibrations of certain sounds even though I couldn't hear them. They felt stronger in my bad ear because there were no signals traveling to my brain from that side to compete for attention. Eventually, after some pretty sophisticated tests, the specialists confirmed what we suspected, zero hearing in my left ear. None. Zip.

Here's why I tell you that – life works the same way.

There's a war for your attention. The world will throw a hundred things at you – not just sounds, but distractions that hit every sense you have. News alerts, work deadlines, phone notifications, endless scrolling, constant noise. It's all designed to keep you from really hearing the stuff that matters.

Psalm 46 talks about a world at war – and then it gives a command that almost feels out of place in the middle of all that chaos:

"Be still, and know that I am God" (Psalm 46:10).

That's not just a suggestion. It's an order.

It reminds me of that moment in the Gospels when Jesus was asleep in the boat while His disciples panicked through a raging storm:

"When Jesus woke up, he rebuked the wind and said to the waves, 'Silence! Be still!' Suddenly the wind stopped, and there was a great calm" (Mark 4:39 NLT).

He didn't shout over the storm. He shut it down.

And here's the thing – there's a storm going on for your mind, your peace, and your soul. But you're not in it alone. You've got a father in heaven who loves you and is on your side. The question is – can you quiet yourself long enough to hear Him?

Paul put it plainly:

"If God is for us, who can be against us" (Romans 8:31)?

Jesus repeated it often, "He that has ears to hear, let him hear." Hearing is more than sound waves – it's focus, attention, and willingness.

And then there's this blessing God told Moses to give His people – a promise that still stands today:

"The Lord bless you and keep you; the Lord make his face shine on you and be gracious to you; the Lord turn his face toward you and give you peace" (Numbers 6:24–26).

That promise is for you too – if you'll turn your face toward Him, the way I turn my good ear toward a voice I need to hear. Look Him straight on. Tune out the noise. Be still.

Because stillness makes room for His voice.

Growth

What noise or distraction is keeping you from hearing God – and how can you be still today?

Grace

Stillness creates space for God's voice to be heard.

Week 5 —
On the Edge

Ted Lode, in *Guerrillas of Grace*, prayed this:

"How shall I pray? Are tears prayer, Lord? Are screams prayers, or groans or sighs or curses? Can trembling hands be lifted to you, or clenched fists, or the cold sweat that trickles down my back, or the cramps that knot my stomach? Will you accept my prayers Lord, my real prayers, rooted in the muck and mud and rock of my life and not just the pretty, cut flower, gracefully arranged bouquet of words? Will you accept me Lord, as I really am, a messed up mixture of glory and grace?"

That's raw. No religious polish. No "just the right words." Just the truth.

Oswald Chambers, in *My Utmost for His Highest*, didn't hold back either:

"If Jesus Christ is to regenerate me, what is the problem He is up against? I have a heredity I had no say in; I am not holy, nor likely to be; and if all Jesus Christ can do is to tell me I must be holy, His teaching only brings despair."

And Rick Warren, in *The Purpose Driven Life* adds:

"…willpower can produce short-term change, but it creates constant internal stress because you haven't dealt with the root cause. The change doesn't feel natural, so eventually you give up and quickly revert to your old habits and hang-ups."

I've been chewing on something lately during my prayer and devotional time. How do lonely, hurting, confused, discouraged people find real, lasting change? Not "I had a good week" change. Not "new year's resolution" change. But life-changing transformation.

Some folks live so close to the edge they can feel it crumbling under their feet. Inches from despair or losing their mind.

Even in church, people sometimes feel more alone – not less. They sit in the pew, look around, and think, I don't belong here. Everybody else has it together.

And then there's the rest of us – swinging between good days and bad, peace and fear, joy and frustration. Watching people we care about get stuck in a cycle of failure, convinced there's no real hope for them.

And then I read this:

"But when this priest had offered for all time one sacrifice for sins, he sat down at the right hand of God… because by one sacrifice he has made perfect forever those who are being made holy" (Hebrews 10:12–14).

Did you catch that? Being made holy.

Jesus already made us perfect in God's sight – but we're still in process. It's not instant. It's a journey.

Paul understood the struggle:

"It happens so regularly that it's predictable. The moment I decide to do good, sin is there to trip me up… I've tried everything and nothing helps. I'm at the end of my rope. Is there no one who can do anything for me?… The answer, thank God, is that Jesus Christ can and does" (Romans 7:21–25 MSG).

That's it right there. The answer isn't "try harder." It's "stay closer."

So what do we actually do about it?

1. Spend time with Him. You can't send your pastor. You can't send your wife. You've got to go yourself. And bring the real you – not the cleaned-up version. God's not looking for the "cut flower bouquet" prayers. He wants the gut-level truth.

2. Follow the map for yourself. The Bible isn't just a book – it's sixty-six books of direction, truth, and encouragement. Read it. Don't just hear about it secondhand.

3. Lean on others. Nobody walks this road alone and makes it far. Find someone you trust, be accountable, and walk together.

4. Rely on God's power. Stop acting like you can fix yourself. You can't. But He can. Ask for help. Ask again tomorrow. Ask again the day after that.

James says it plainly:

"You do not have because you do not ask God" (James 4:2b).

And Paul prayed it this way:

"Since the day we heard about you, we have not stopped praying for you… that you may live a life worthy of the Lord… being strengthened with all power according to his glorious might…" (Colossians 1:9–11).

The bottom line? Lasting change isn't about grit – it's about connection. The closer you stay to Him, the more He changes you from the inside out.

Growth

Where are you trying to change yourself by willpower alone – and what might happen if you asked God for help instead?

Grace

The power to change doesn't come from trying harder – it comes from staying closer.

Week 6 —
Weeds

"This means that anyone who belongs to Christ has become a new person. The old life is gone; a new life has begun" (2 Corinthians 5:17 NLT)!

The first time I seriously thought about suicide was on the way home from a job I had grown to hate, heading toward a family I'd let down and could barely look in the eye anymore.

Driving those lonely, back-country mountain roads, I realized something that scared me – I could find my way to dead real easy.

Why now? I'd been through hard times before – layoffs and recession in the Midwest in the '80s, struggling to make it as a photographer in Phoenix, even watching a business partnership in Greensboro go sideways. Not once in those times did I think about ending it.

I think it was the weeds.

See, my mom had given me the greatest gift – hope. She didn't have an easy past herself (troubled, reckless, even criminal at times), but she poured encouragement into me. When I failed, when I was heartbroken, she'd say, "One day it will be your day." Thanks to her, I grew up believing there was always a reason to get back up.

But over the years, the weeds started coming in. Slowly at first. I let things that didn't matter much take over – status, stuff, trying to impress certain people. I went from being the guy who loved being with his wife and kids to being the guy devoted to work, hobbies, and whatever distracted me from what was important.

Somewhere along the way, I started feeling sorry for myself – deciding I was done being last and it was time to put myself first.

Then my mom died. Not long after, my sister – my best friend – died too. Cancer. In losing them, I lost the two most hopeful, loving voices in my life.

I blamed God. Figured He'd fallen asleep at the wheel. Why let people like me keep breathing while they were gone?

So I walked away from Him. Didn't look back. And eventually, I found myself alone – completely, hopelessly alone.

That's when the thought showed up. And then again. And again. Pretty soon, I wasn't just thinking about it – I was planning.

But then something strange happened. In a moment of clarity, I thought, *If I'm better off dead, then maybe I might as well give life one last shot.* Worst-case scenario, I figured, I'd end up back in the weeds – with no regrets about trying.

So I tried.

For a long time, I wandered, looking for hope. Then it came – unexpectedly – through a friend of a friend who invited me to something. Next thing I knew, I was back in a church. Back in homes where laughter, faith, and grace were alive. Around people who had found their way back to hope – and were willing to walk with me until I did too.

At first, I battled the voices in my head telling me I'd gone too far, hurt too many, wasted too much, used up all my chances.

But over time, another voice broke through – quieter, steadier. Full of love. Full of mercy. Full of forgiveness.

Little by little, Jesus started pulling up the weeds – pain, fear, regret, selfishness. And in the bare spots, He planted new things. Healing. Peace. Real joy.

If you feel overrun with weeds – mistakes, loss, bitterness – hear this, you're not too far gone. God hasn't given up on you. He's not afraid of your mess. And He's a master at turning overgrown, dried-up ground into a garden.

All you have to do is hand Him the field.

Growth

What weeds have crept into your life – what needs to be pulled so God's healing can begin?

Grace

You may feel overgrown by sorrow and failure, but God hasn't given up on you. Let Him pull the weeds and plant new life.

Week 7 — *True Valentine*

When I think of Valentine's Day, I confess I get a bit uncomfortable – "squirmish," even. I love my wife and don't shy away from spoiling her when I can, but I've never been completely at ease with the way culture celebrates the day. Chocolates, flowers, heartfelt notes, and fancy dinners are fine – I've given them and received them – but something in me always feels like there's more to love than a red box of candy and a Hallmark card.

That's why Valentine's Day often becomes a moment of reflection for me. Beneath the roses and ribbon, it's an opportunity to think about the deeper essence of love – not just the romantic kind, but the kind that echoes the selfless, sacrificial love of God.

John 15:13 captures this beautifully:

"No greater love has any man than this, that he lay down his life for his friends."

When Jesus said those words, He wasn't talking about buying gifts or writing poems. He was pointing to the cross. He defined love not as a fleeting emotion or a grand romantic gesture, but as sacrifice. And that's the part we often forget.

I once heard a story about a husband who woke up at 4:30 every morning to make coffee and breakfast for his wife before she headed to work. He didn't do it for recognition or to post about it on Instagram – he just did it because he loved her. Another friend told me about his mom who slept in a chair beside his hospital bed for three nights in a row, refusing to leave until she knew he was safe. I think of a neighbor who quietly drives an elderly widow to her appointments every week, never asking for gas money, never making a big deal of it.

Those things may not look like Valentine's Day romance, but they are the truest expressions of love – sacrifice in the small things.

Paul wrote in 1 Corinthians 13:

"Love is patient, love is kind… It always protects, always trusts, always hopes, always perseveres. Love never fails."

Notice how he doesn't say anything about flowers, chocolates, or candlelit dinners. Not that those things are bad – they can be wonderful – but they're not the test of love. True love is revealed when it costs us something, our time, our pride, our comfort, sometimes even our dreams.

That's why I think it's worth remembering the origins of Valentine's Day. Long before it became a holiday of romance, it was about a man named Valentine – a Christian priest in Rome who lived in the third century. When Emperor Claudius outlawed marriage for young soldiers (believing single men fought better), Valentine defied the decree and secretly married couples in the church. When his actions were discovered, he was arrested and eventually executed. His

"Valentine's" gift wasn't roses – it was his life, laid down for his faith and for love.

And here's the connection that matters most, Jesus did the same for us. He gave up the glory of heaven, lived humbly, and willingly laid down His life so that we might live. That's the love that never fails.

So this Valentine's Day, I'll still buy a card for my wife and probably sneak some chocolate her way. I'll still take her out to dinner or try to do something special. But more importantly, I'll remember that love isn't about what I can get – it's about what I'm willing to give.

And I'll ask myself the same question I'll ask you, Am I showing the kind of love that reflects the heart of Christ? Not just in February, not just in romance, but in daily sacrifice – the coffee made, the child comforted, the neighbor helped, the friend encouraged?

Because when it's all said and done, true Valentine's love isn't measured in gifts. It's measured in giving.

Growth

How can you express a deeper, more sacrificial love to someone in your life this week?

Grace

True love is measured not by what we receive, but by what we are willing to give.

Week 8 —
Ancient of Days

Old is relative.

When I was a kid, I thought teenagers were ancient – full-grown adults who could do whatever they wanted. Then I became a teenager and decided real life started when I could do whatever I wanted with no rules. That day came and went… and eventually I started thinking, *Maybe I just need to get a little older and wiser, so I'll stop doing so much stupid stuff.*

Well, here I am, "older and wiser," and guess what? I still do stupid stuff pretty regularly. So when exactly is "old enough" old enough? And when does that promised wisdom kick in?

Maybe "old" is just as relative as "wise." Some things do seem to get better with age – classic cars, fine wine, cheddar cheese, cast iron skillets, leather, fishing stories, and maybe a few friendships. Other things… not so much.

I do think we can get better with age, but it doesn't just happen because more birthdays pile up. It takes effort, some solid choices, and one more thing I'll get to in a minute.

We can work at things that make aging better – stuff like self-confidence, empathy, better decision-making, stronger friendships, healthier family relationships, and even better communication skills. Those don't automatically show up just because you've got more candles on the cake.

Case in point, I recently went through a well-known marriage counseling training for my church. One of the first exercises was to choose three communication skills I wanted to improve. My top three?

1. Holding my opinion until the right time.

2. Coming across as warmer in conversations.

3. Showing more genuine interest in others.

All good things. But here's the kicker – wanting to change doesn't make it happen. Changing yourself is hard.

Max Lucado, in his book, *He Still Moves Stones*, says this about aging:

"You can take the safe route, or you can hear the voice of God's adventure. Follow God's impulses. Adopt the child. Move overseas. Teach the class. Change careers. Make a difference. Your last chapters can be your best chapters. God's oldest have always been among his choicest."

Those last words – *God's oldest...* – are the key. Maybe even just that one word: *God's.*

If you want to age well, start there. Are you His? Does He own your heart?

If not, it's never too late. My dad was a stubborn old guy. Physical handicap or not, he wouldn't ask for help. Didn't want charity. Always claimed he had things under control – and when it was clear he didn't, he let you know with a few choice words.

But all that changed the day we buried my sister. She was only forty-three. That day my dad realized we have a whole lot less control over our lives than we like to think. That day he gave his heart to the Lord – at the ripe old age of 72.

So, no – you're never too old to get better. But the first step is to stop going it alone. Let the One who's been there all along lead you in the right direction.

That next step you take? It could be the first one toward a brand-new kind of life. Trust the King of your life. And then, when old age rolls in, you can tell it exactly where to go.

"In my vision at night I looked, and there before me was one like a son of man, coming with the clouds of heaven. He approached the Ancient of Days and was led into his presence. He was given authority, glory and sovereign power; all nations and peoples of every language worshipped him. His dominion is an everlasting dominion that will not pass away, and his kingdom is one that will never be destroyed" (Daniel 7:13–14).

Growth

Where in your life are you "going it alone" instead of letting God lead – and what's keeping you from handing it over to Him?

Grace

You're never too old to start new – but start with Him.

Stage 2

Wrestling & Awakening

Week 9 — *Horse Sense*

The cowboy was barely holding on. Slumped in the saddle, baked by two days of desert heat, he and his horse had been without food or water long enough to feel like they were running on fumes. Every step over rocks and cacti was slow, heavy, and painful.

They were heading toward what might be their last shot at survival – a spring called *Occults del Agua*, or Hidden Water. Old-timers swore it existed, but finding it was another story. And today, with the cowboy chased into the mountains by rustlers, surviving only with his horse and his life, the odds weren't great.

Then, out of nowhere, the horse's head snapped up. Its ears locked forward. A burst of energy shot through it. The cowboy was barely hanging on as the horse lunged ahead. When it skidded to a sudden stop at a dry wash, the cowboy went flying over its head, landing hard.

Still clutching the reins, he was about to scold the horse when he saw it – sunlight flashing off a pool of clear water. His heart leaped. This had to be the Hidden Spring.

Mumbling thanks to both his horse and the old prospector who'd told him about it, he stepped forward. But the horse jerked back hard, snorting and pawing at the ground, refusing to move closer.

Frustrated, the cowboy dropped the reins and stepped toward the water. That's when he saw them – bones. Mule deer. Coyotes. Even a jackrabbit.

This wasn't Hidden Water. This was poison.

If you've watched enough westerns, you know the lesson – sometimes the horse has more sense than the rider. Horses can smell bad water.

Here's the thing – life is full of "watering holes" that look good but will wreck you if you drink from them. Spiritually speaking, there's no shortage of bad water these days. Some of it's sold by slick talkers with bad intentions. Some of it's offered by well-meaning folks who are just wrong. Either way, the result's the same – it'll leave you worse off than before.

The Bible warns us about this kind of thing – false teaching, empty promises, self-help without God. And let's be honest, the church has given skeptics reasons to doubt. Hypocrisy. Scandals. People talking about Jesus but living nothing like Him. If you've ever thought, *I'm not drinking what they're selling,* I get it.

But here's the difference – when you've developed spiritual horse sense, you can smell the bad water before you drink it. And you can find the good water – the only real water – that will actually satisfy.

That's what Jesus offered a woman at a well one hot afternoon:

"Everyone who drinks this water will be thirsty again, but whoever drinks the water I give them will never thirst. Indeed, the water I give them will become in them a spring of water welling up to eternal life" (John 4:13–14).

That's living water – straight from the source. Not through a person, a movement, or a trend. Just Him.

So here's some cowboy advice for your soul:

- Don't drink just because you're thirsty. Test the water first.

- Don't assume every "spring" is safe. Look for the bones.

- Don't ignore the warnings – especially from the One who knows better.

Develop spiritual horse sense. Learn to tell the difference between something that looks refreshing but poisons your soul and the living water Jesus offers.

When you stick close to Him, you won't just avoid bad water – you'll find yourself drinking from the one well that never runs dry.

Growth

Where in your life have you been drinking from a source that leaves you thirstier instead of filled – and what would it take to develop the spiritual horse sense to tell the difference?

Grace

Bad water is everywhere. Stick close to Jesus, and you'll have the horse sense to know the difference.

Week 10 —
5 + 2 = 5000 (With 12 Left Over)

Philip had to be thinking, *"Jesus, you've lost it."*

They were surrounded by a massive crowd – five thousand men, plus women and kids. People had been listening to Jesus teach all day. They were tired. They were hungry. And then Jesus turns to Philip and basically says, "So… where do we buy bread for all these people?"

Philip's answer? "It would take more than half a year's wages to buy enough bread for each one to have a bite" (John 6:7)!

Translation: *This is impossible. We don't have it.*

And Philip wasn't wrong – at least not mathematically. But Jesus wasn't running the same numbers. He already knew how this was going to go down. As He'd said elsewhere, "With man this is impossible, but not with God; all things are possible with God" (Mark 10:27).

Then along comes a kid with his lunch – five loaves and two fish. Not a catering order. Not even a Costco-sized family pack. More like a couple biscuits and two sardines.

Jesus takes the food, prays over it, and hands it to the disciples to start passing out. And it just… doesn't… run out. Everybody eats until they're full. Then the disciples go around and pick up twelve baskets of leftovers.

That's twelve baskets – after starting with one lunch.

Mark Batterson, in *Circle Maker: Praying Circles Around Your Biggest Dreams and Greatest Fears*, says the point is that where we see limits, God sees opportunity. We say, "I can't." God says, "Watch Me."

So what does that mean for us? First, it means we can stop pretending we've got it all handled. You can't feed five thousand people. You can't fix every broken thing in the world. You can't heal the sick or raise the dead. You can't even handle every problem in your own life.

But God can.

In His math, five plus two doesn't equal seven – it equals five thousand... with twelve baskets left over.

And here's the kicker, Jesus says we're invited into that same work.

"I tell you the truth, anyone who believes in me will do the same works I have done, and even greater works, because I am going to be with the Father. You can ask for anything in my name, and I will do it, so that the Son can bring glory to the Father (John 14:12–13 NLT)."

Let's break that down:

1. "I will do..." – He's the one making it happen.

2. "You can ask for anything in my name..." – Our job is to ask.

But a lot of us don't ask like we believe that. We pray small, safe prayers just in case God doesn't come through – because if He doesn't, we don't want to be disappointed.

Here's the thing – faith isn't hedging your bets. Faith is showing up with the whole lunch.

That kid didn't give Jesus one loaf and say, "Better keep the rest for me." He handed it all over. And that's when the miracle happened.

So what's in your "lunch" right now? A little time? A little money? A skill you think isn't worth much? You might be looking at it thinking, *This won't even make a dent.* But God's looking at it thinking, *Perfect.*

The way it works is simple, you bring what you've got, and you let Him handle the multiplying. That's not your job. Your job is to hand it over and get out of the way.

And when you do, don't be surprised if He gives you more than you asked for. That's His style. He didn't just feed the crowd that day – He sent His disciples home hauling twelve baskets of leftovers.

So stop measuring what's possible by what's in your hand. Start measuring it by Who's holding it.

Because in His hands, 5 + 2 will always be more than enough.

"With man this is impossible, but not with God; all things are possible with God" (Mark 10:27).

Growth

Where have you been relying on your own strength instead of asking God to do what only He can?

Grace

God delights in doing the impossible – especially when we bring Him our not-enough.

Week 11 —
Hope Springs Eternal

"With man this is impossible, but with God all things are possible" (Matthew 19:26).

"What a wretched man I am! Who will rescue me from this body that is subject to death? Thanks be to God, who delivers me through Jesus Christ our Lord!" (Romans 7:24-25).

What a week it was.

Ever have one of those? The kind where nothing seems to go right? I (usually) start with the best of intentions, but sometimes no matter what I do, I can't seem to please anyone. It wasn't one huge catastrophe – more like a winter storm of little frustrations and failures piling up until the weight just sat heavy.

If I'm being honest, I don't handle rejection well. And this week stirred up old memories of rejection – some unfair, some that I absolutely earned. That's the thing about rejection, it doesn't just bruise your ego in the moment. It echoes. It drags old failures up from the basement of your memory and parades them in front of you.

One night, I sat down and started making a list of my failures. Not just the recent ones, but all of them I could remember. Four single-spaced pages later, I stopped. The last line I typed was short and brutal, "Failure at everything…"

I'm not telling you this to fish for pity. I'm telling you because honesty matters. And the truth is, I get stuck in those failures sometimes. Some of them are so vivid I still break out in a cold sweat just thinking about them.

But something strange happened as I sat staring at that "Failures List." I couldn't bring myself to hit "Save." My fingers hovered over the keyboard, frozen. And then, like a flicker of firelight in the middle of a dark night, I felt, more than heard, a whisper:

"With man this is impossible, but with God all things are possible."

I had to look it up. It's what Jesus told His disciples in Matthew 19 when they asked, "Who then can be saved?"

Those words hit me like cold water to the face. Who can be saved? Not the guy who just typed out four pages of failure. Not the one who keeps circling back to the same mistakes. Not me.

But Jesus says, "Yes, you. Even you."

With man, impossible. With God, possible.

Psalm 103 puts it like this:

"The Lord is compassionate and gracious, slow to anger, abounding in love... He does not treat us as our sins deserve... as far as the east is from the west, so far has he removed our transgressions from us."

David wrote that. The same David who messed up more than once – publicly, painfully – but kept coming back to God. A man who knew failure intimately and grace even more so.

That's what hope looks like. Not denial of the mess. Not pretending the failure doesn't matter. But hearing God say, "I know. And I forgive you anyway."

Romans 7 makes it even plainer. Paul, one of the greatest apostles, admits, "What a wretched man I am!" Then he asks the question that has kept me up plenty of nights, "Who will rescue me?"

And he answers it, "Thanks be to God, who delivers me through Jesus Christ our Lord!"

That's the point. We can't rescue ourselves. We can't erase our past. We can't balance the scales by trying harder.

But we don't have to. God already has.

Through Jesus, the impossible becomes possible.

Growth

What failures from your past still haunt you? Have you been trying to "balance the scales" on your own?

Grace

You can't erase the past – but you don't have to. God already has. Through Jesus, the impossible becomes possible.

Week 12 —
A Legacy of Love

"I thank my God every time I remember you" (Philippians 1:3).

Three simple words – *I remember you* – can carry the weight of a lifetime. They can bridge years, miles, even oceans. They can come in a letter, a text, a phone call, or a quiet prayer whispered in the dark. And when they do, they speak to something every heart longs for, a legacy.

Nobody wants to be forgotten. No one hopes to fade into obscurity, becoming a faint shadow of who they once were – like the worn, barely legible words on an old tombstone. Who lies here? What was their story? Did they matter? Were they loved?

I think back to March 2021, when we were finalizing the twelfth issue of our magazine since the world had been upended by a global pandemic. It had been a year of loss like nothing most of us had ever seen. Friends, acquaintances, and family members gone far too soon. And the strangest part? We couldn't even mourn together the way we always had.

Funerals postponed or held online. Hugs withheld. Grief carried alone. Tears that came suddenly and hard, like a flash flood rushing through a dry canyon.

Moses knew what that felt like:

"You turn people back to dust, saying, 'Return to dust, you mortals.'

A thousand years in your sight are like a day that has just gone by,

or like a watch in the night.

Yet you sweep people away in the sleep of death – they are like the new grass of the morning: In the morning it springs up new, but by evening it is dry and withered" (Psalm 90:3-6).

In those days, it felt like we were all being forced to confront our own mortality. Even the young weren't spared.

Around that time, I heard a college professor speak in chapel. His message was short but powerful. He called it *Outlive Your Death*. His challenge was simple – live in such a way that your influence, your love, and your impact outlast your years.

That stuck with me.

Moses prayed it this way:

"Teach us to number our days, that we may gain a heart of wisdom" (Psalm 90:12).

Wisdom teaches us to live intentionally – to know that every moment, every word, every act of kindness shapes how we'll be remembered.

Even an insurance company gets this. I once stumbled across an article on their site (not where I expected spiritual insight) that said:

"A lasting legacy is all about the actions you take during your life and the way those actions affect how people remember you... to ensure your loved ones will be taken care of when you're gone, and always remember you with love."

Practical? Sure. But here's the truth, no financial legacy lasts forever. Wealth fades. Possessions scatter. Names get lost to history.

The only legacy that truly endures is a legacy of love.

John put it simply, "God is love." His love is eternal, and through Jesus Christ, that love is offered to every one of us. It's the love we're called to both receive and pass on. The love we live out – in our families, friendships, workplaces, and communities – is the one thing that will ripple beyond our lifetime.

Moses closed Psalm 90 with this prayer:

"May your deeds be shown to your servants,

your splendor to their children.

May the favor of the Lord our God rest on us;

establish the work of our hands for us –

yes, establish the work of our hands (Psalm 90:16-17)."

If we live with love as our foundation, we can trust God to establish the work of our hands in ways that outlive our days. And when someone, somewhere, whispers *I remember you*, it will be because love left a mark they couldn't forget.

Growth

If your life ended today, what would those closest to you remember most? What intentional steps can you take now to leave a legacy of love?

Grace

The only legacy that lasts forever is a legacy of love.

Week 13 —
Don't Lose Your Head

When my sister and I were kids, we spent a chunk of our summers with relatives in Tennessee and the Carolinas. Life there was slower... until it wasn't.

One day, we were outside playing when one of our aunts stepped out to "fix dinner." And when I say "fix dinner," I don't mean she preheated the oven. I mean she walked outside, grabbed a rooster, and headed for the woodpile.

One quick swing of the hatchet and... well... let's just say that rooster was no longer a going to crow when the sun rose next.

But here's the part that still lives in family legend – the part that had my sister swearing off poultry for the evening. The bird, now headless, took off running. Full speed. Spewing blood. Crashing into fence posts, trees, anything in the way – including my screaming sister.

I'll be honest – I laughed. Hilariously. Tears even. But the picture stuck with me.

That rooster had no clue it was already dead. It was all instinct and reflex – pure motion without any meaning behind it.

Ever feel like that?

Like you're running hard, bumping into everything and everyone, staying constantly in motion – but completely disconnected from why you're doing what you're doing?

I've been there. More times than I'd like to admit.

That's why Colossians 2:19 hits me like a two-by-four:

"He has lost connection with the head, from whom the whole body, supported and held together by its ligaments and sinews, grows as God causes it to grow."

When we lose connection with *the* head – Jesus – we're just flapping and thrashing, burning energy but going nowhere that matters.

Jesus put it this way:

"I am the vine; you are the branches... apart from me you can do nothing" (John 15:5).

Not "apart from me you can do a little" or "you can do okay on your own." Nothing.

So how do we stay connected?

For me, it means staying active in the life of Christ – not just believing He exists, but actually participating in what He's doing. Jesus gave us the blueprint:

"Love each other as I have loved you" (John 15:12b).

That's where it starts.

Sometimes we overfeed on sermons, devotionals, podcasts, and Bible studies, but we never actually move. It's like eating all day but never getting off the couch. Eventually, our faith turns into spiritual couch potato mode – lots of input, no output. We forget the mission.

Paul gave this challenge:

"Set your hearts on things above, where Christ is... Set your minds on things above, not on earthly things" (Colossians 3:1–2).

That's not just a "think happy thoughts" verse – it's a call to aim your life higher than your to-do list, higher than your comfort zone, higher than your own agenda.

Here's what I've learned about staying connected:

- Stay close to Jesus. Prayer, Scripture, worship, time with other believers – it's how you keep the signal strong.

- Bear fruit. Real fruit. Not just warm fuzzies. Jesus said love isn't just a feeling – it's action.

- Love boldly. Take the risk. Make the call. Write the note. Carry the groceries. Send the prayer.

Jesus didn't leave us guessing what love looks like:

"Greater love has no one than this: to lay down one's life for one's friends" (John 15:13).

Paul echoed it:

"The only thing that counts is faith expressing itself through love" (Galatians 5:6b).

Growth

Are you moving with meaning – or just motion? What helps you stay connected to the true source?

Grace

Don't lose your head. Life without Jesus is just a lot of noise and flapping.

Week 14 —
Mr. Doesn't Matter

There's a line in an old western I've always liked. A small-town dentist asks a gunfighter, played by John Wayne, his name. "Doesn't matter," the gunfighter mutters. "Well Mr. Doesn't Matter, I hope you can do something," the dentist replies. That line has stuck with me for years. Maybe because, deep down, I've often felt like *Mr. Doesn't Matter* myself. Not in a hopeless way – but in the way that reminds me that what really matters isn't my name, my reputation, or whether I get the credit. What matters is whether I'm willing to show up and let God work through me.

There have been plenty of times I've looked at someone hurting – someone who feels invisible, overlooked, or forgotten – and that line echoes in my head. "Well Mr. Doesn't Matter, I hope you can do something." And the truth is, I can't. Not really. Not on my own. I'm not the hero of this story. I'm not the answer. I'm just a vessel. A flawed one, sure, but still one God can pour something through. The apostle Paul put it this way, "But we have this treasure in jars of clay to show that this all-surpassing power is from God and not from us" (2 Corinthians 4:7). We're the jars. He's the treasure. That takes the pressure off, doesn't it? God doesn't need perfection. He needs obedience. He doesn't need stars. He needs servants. He doesn't even need the jar to be beautiful or polished. He just needs it to be available.

That's humbling. Because sometimes I've tried to help and only made things worse. Other times I've hesitated, afraid I'd mess it up, afraid I'd say the wrong thing, or afraid I'd fail. But here's what I'm learning, failure isn't final when God is involved. He doesn't waste it. He shapes us through it. And He sees us – even when we feel like nobodies. "Are not five sparrows sold for two pennies? Yet not one of them is forgotten by God. Indeed, the very hairs of your head are all numbered. Don't be afraid; you are worth more than many sparrows" (Luke 12:6–7). If He sees sparrows, He sees you.

So my prayer has become simple, God, don't let me get hardened or disillusioned. Don't let me dry out. Keep shaping me into someone more like Jesus – compassionate, humble, and available. Because being available matters more than being impressive. Think about the people Jesus chose: fishermen, a tax collector, zealots, doubters, ordinary men with ordinary lives. Their resumes didn't matter. Their willingness did. And the same is true for us. So when you're tempted to think you don't matter, remember this, you do. Not because of your name, your success, or your reputation, but because of the God who chooses to work through you.

God doesn't need stars. He needs servants. Sometimes the best thing we can do is simply get out of the way so His love can shine through. So yeah – "Mr. Doesn't Matter." That's me. But if God can use a nobody like me to reach somebody He loves, then maybe "Mr. Doesn't Matter" actually does matter after all. Not because of who I am. But because of who He is.

Growth

What would change if you saw yourself not as the solution, but as the vessel through which God brings the solution?

Grace

It's not about being important – it's about being available.

Week 15 —
Roots

Thunderstorms in the mountains where I live don't usually compare to the ones that rip across the flatlands, but every so often a storm blows through that makes you sit up straight and pay attention. Years ago, one of those storms rolled in with enough force to take down trees, scatter branches, and rattle windows. When the skies finally cleared, the kids and I took a walk and noticed a mature apple tree nearby lying on its side – completely uprooted. It had been standing tall that morning, just beginning to bloom with the promise of fruit. But by evening, its roots were exposed, its blossoms scattered like confetti, and a small clump of clay clung stubbornly to the base as if refusing to admit what had just happened.

I remember shaking my head and telling my kids, "It's a shame to lose such a big apple tree. The deer will miss feeding off it this year." But, as it turns out, I was wrong.

That summer, the tree still produced apples. Big ones too. Not the shriveled, twisted kind you might expect from a tree lying sideways and half-dead, but full-sized, healthy fruit. The combination of heavy rainfall, just enough soil still clinging to the roots, and the tree's own stored-up strength allowed it to produce one final harvest. The local deer were thrilled – they didn't even have to stretch to reach the fruit. For a season, the tree looked alive, even fruitful.

But when fall came, the truth could no longer be hidden. Its leaves withered and fell, and by winter the weight of snow finished what the storm had started. The following spring, new growth popped up all around the valley – but not from that tree. Its last crop had been its farewell. Before long, someone came by, cut it into sections, and split it for firewood. It had looked alive for a season. But in reality, it had died the day the storm uprooted it.

That image has stayed with me, because I've come to realize how much like that tree we can be. Storms hit all of us – storms of divorce, depression, failure, addiction, betrayal, or sometimes just the slow, soul-numbing drift of apathy. The impact knocks us over, and though we may still look okay for a while, something vital has shifted beneath the surface. We might keep moving, keep producing, keep pretending, but if our roots have been pulled from the source of life, the countdown has already begun.

That's what happened in the Garden of Eden. God told Adam and Eve that the moment they ate from the forbidden tree, they would surely die. But they didn't keel over on the spot. They lived long lives, raised children, and kept going. On the surface, they looked alive. But in that moment of disobedience, their roots had been ripped from the source of life. Death – spiritual death – had already begun. It just took time to show.

That's the danger for us too. We can be disconnected from God and not even realize it. We can keep going through the motions – working, parenting, even serving in church – and fool ourselves into thinking we're fine. But inside, we've lost contact with the root system. The life force. The vine.

Jesus didn't mince words when He said, "Remain in me, and I will remain in you. For a branch cannot produce fruit if it is severed from the vine… For apart from me you can do nothing" (John 15:4–5 NLT). That's not poetic imagery. It's spiritual biology. No roots, no life. No connection, no fruit.

The good news is, if you're reading this, you're not firewood yet. You're not beyond hope. Even if you've been living off yesterday's faith, yesterday's connection, or yesterday's strength, you can return. You can dig back in. The same storms that tried to tear you out can drive your roots deeper – if you let them push you toward the vine instead of away.

So don't just survive. Don't just cling to the appearance of life. Abide. Stay connected. Hold fast to Jesus, the only source of life that doesn't dry up. Because with Him, even after the worst storm, new life is possible.

Growth

Have you been living off yesterday's connection with God? What would it look like to abide deeply in Him again?

Grace

It's not how alive you look – it's whether you're rooted in the One who gives life.

Week 16 —
Beloved

I've always loved concerts. Rock, jazz, classical, Christian rock – you name it. There's something about the energy of a live show – the lights, the sound, the crowd moving as one. It's electric, almost intoxicating. When the band's locked in and the music hits your chest harder than the speakers, it feels like being alive in a way little else does.

One night before I was married, I went to a concert with a buddy. It started like a lot of nights out – grabbing drinks beforehand at a nearby bar. Neither of us were heavy drinkers, but that night we had just enough to soften the edges, loosen the mood, and dull the filter. By the time we made our way into the concert hall, the music was thumping, the crowd was swaying, and we were primed for fun.

It was wall-to-wall people, the kind of crowd where you could barely lift your arms without bumping into somebody. I got lost in it – the movement, the bass rattling my bones, the lights flashing across a sea of strangers. Then, through the chaos, I noticed her.

Not first because of her looks, though she was striking – but because of the commotion she was caught in. A much larger, very drunk woman was in her face, yelling, shoving, hurling insults. The smaller woman shoved her way out of it and pushed through the crowd, her eyes darting until, somehow, they locked on mine. Thirty people between us, thousands around us, and yet in that instant it felt like we were the only two in the room.

When she finally broke free and reached me, she leaned in and shouted in my ear over the music, "That lady was crazy!" Then she pressed herself against me, dancing in rhythm with the pounding beat, pulling me into her orbit before I even knew what was happening.

I won't sugarcoat it – I was drunk on more than just beer. I was drunk on attention, on desire, on the thrill of being noticed. Chosen. For a moment, I felt the rush of temptation wash over me, warm and reckless. And that's when it happened.

A voice.

"She is my daughter."

Startled, I jerked my head around to see who had spoken. Nobody. Just the mass of bodies moving to the music, oblivious.

"She is my daughter," the voice repeated, firmer this time.

Again I turned. Still no one. And then came the third statement, clear as a strike of lightning, steady as a heartbeat:

"I am your Father. And she is my daughter. See her as I see her."

Everything in me shifted in that moment. The haze lifted. I looked at this woman – this stranger who moments ago I had seen as a chance, a thrill, a fleeting conquest – and I saw her differently. Not as an object. Not as an opportunity. But as a soul. A daughter. His daughter. A person loved by the Father I claimed to follow, whether she knew Him or not.

She kept dancing, unaware of the war that had just ended inside me. When she opened her eyes and noticed my expression had changed, she pulled back a little and asked, "What is it?"

"Where were you headed?" I asked.

"To the bathroom." She laughed. "Do you know how to get out of here?"

I helped her push through the crowd, found the staircase, and pointed the way. She kissed me quickly on the mouth, smiled, and disappeared up the steps. Just like that, she was gone.

But the voice stayed. "Love her. Love them all. As I love them."

I returned to my friend, but the music no longer had the same pull. The lights, the noise, the crowd – it all seemed thinner, less real. I stood there in the middle of a sold-out show, stone sober, my heart pounding with something far greater than adrenaline. I prayed for her – for her safety, her identity, her worth. And I prayed for myself – that I would see every person who crossed my path not through my own selfish lens, but through the eyes of the Father.

Because the truth is, every person you lock eyes with carries the same label, "Beloved child." And if we don't see them that way, we're missing the very heart of God.

Growth

Who are you seeing today only through your own eyes? What would it mean to see them as God's beloved child instead?

Grace

Before you reach for someone, remember whose child they are. Love them as He loves them.

Stage 3

Surrender & Freedom

Week 17 — *Soul Food*

Full confession, I struggle with making healthy food choices. Always have. I grew up in a dessert-loving family where junk food wasn't a treat – it was a staple. Ice cream, cookies, chips, soda – if sugar or salt was involved, it was probably on the table. To this day, I can walk past a salad bar without a second glance but find myself mysteriously drawn to the snack aisle at the grocery store.

But if I'm being honest, it goes deeper than food. Because what I've noticed is this, my physical appetite often mirrors my spiritual appetite. And too often, I crave junk.

The apostle Paul nailed this problem in his letter to the Philippians. He wrote with tears in his eyes that many people live as "enemies of the cross," with their god being their appetite. He said, "They are headed for destruction. Their god is their appetite, they brag about shameful things, and they think only about this life here on earth" (Philippians 3:19 NLT).

That stings. Because as much as I want to distance myself from that description, I see my reflection in it sometimes. I binge on distractions – social media scrolling, endless entertainment, hobbies, work, news. None of those things are necessarily bad on their own, but when they become my go-to, they numb instead of nourish. And over time, they leave me feeling spiritually bloated, sluggish, and disconnected from what really matters.

Jesus pointed us to something better. After a powerful conversation with a Samaritan woman at a well – a moment that sparked transformation in her entire community – His disciples urged Him to eat something. But He said, "I have a kind of food you know nothing about." They were confused, probably thinking someone had snuck Him a sandwich. But He explained, "My nourishment comes from doing the will of God, who sent me, and from finishing His work" (John 4:34 NLT).

That's soul food. Not the fried chicken-and-mac-n-cheese kind (though I do love that too), but the kind of food that doesn't just fill you up for a moment – it strengthens you, fuels you, and satisfies you at the deepest level.

So why don't I always go after that? Why do I settle for spiritual junk food?

Sometimes it's laziness. Sometimes it's fear – I don't actually want to ask God what He wants, because He might tell me something uncomfortable. Other times it's just habit. I fill my life with noise, and in the process, I starve my soul.

Jesus showed us how to resist that trap. When Satan tempted Him in the wilderness, He was starving – forty days without food. If there was ever a moment where turning stones into bread seemed reasonable, that was it. But Jesus responded with words straight from Deuteronomy, "People do not live by bread alone; rather, we live by every word that comes from the mouth of the Lord" (Deuteronomy 8:3 NLT).

That verse reminds me, I don't live on likes or views. I don't live on comfort or distraction. I don't live on Netflix binges or fast-food faith. I live – really live – on the Word and the will of God.

And here's the thing. When you taste that kind of food, joy follows. Not shallow, sugar-rush joy, but the deep, sustaining kind. The kind Jesus talked about when He said, "The harvesters are paid good wages, and the fruit they harvest is people brought to eternal life. What joy awaits both the planter and the harvester alike!" (John 4:36 NLT).

That's the kind of joy no dessert, no distraction, no junk food of the soul can ever deliver.

So yeah, I'll probably keep fighting the snack aisle at the grocery store. But more importantly, I want to fight the temptation to live on spiritual junk food. Because only God's word, His presence, and His work can truly feed me. That's the soul food I need.

Growth

What are you feeding your soul these days – and is it really nourishing you?

Grace

True soul food is found in doing the will of God. Nothing else satisfies like that.

Week 18 — *Lock and Key*

Freedom. It sounds so good on the surface, doesn't it? The word feels big, bold, and clean. We say we're free. We live in a free country. We're not a slave to any man or anything.

But in our heart of hearts… do we really believe that's true?

Be honest – what holds you captive?

Maybe it's the stuff everybody recognizes as chains, addiction to drugs, alcohol, pornography, sex.

Maybe it's something less obvious that slips under the radar, junk food, endless entertainment, debt, hours of gaming.

Maybe it's a diversion that looks harmless – shopping sprees, soaking up drama, doom-scrolling social media, obsessing over politics.

Or maybe it's something deeper and harder to name, fear, worry, depression, shame, control.

For some, it's the wounds that never fully healed – being broken, hurt, sick, abused.

So again… what has made you its slave?

Freedom sounds great, but maybe we're not as free as we want people to think. Maybe when we're alone with our thoughts, we're not even sure we can be free.

And if that's you, I need you to hear this:

That feeling – that voice in your head saying you'll never change, you'll never get out, you'll never be different – is lying to you. It's not just wrong; it's the actual lock on the prison you're sitting in.

And there's a key.

"You shall know the truth, and the truth shall make you free" (John 8:32 NKJV).

"The Spirit of the Lord is on me… to proclaim freedom for the prisoners" (Luke 4:18).

Jesus doesn't just know where the key is – He *is* the key.

"I am the living one. I died, but look – I am alive forever and ever! And I hold the keys of death and the grave" (Revelation 1:17–18 NLT).

Now, you might be thinking, *But I'm already a Christian. I believe all this – and I'm still stuck.*

You're not alone. Most of us can say that. We trust Jesus with our eternity, but we keep parts of our everyday life locked away.

That's where the challenge comes in. Don't give up.

Bang on that door. I mean it. Whatever it is – lies, habits, fears, distractions, pain – keep pounding until it opens. Pray hard. Pray often. Refuse to settle for anything less than the freedom Christ already purchased for you.

"Here I am! I stand at the door and knock" (Revelation 3:20).

That verse isn't just about salvation – it's also about letting Him into the rooms we've closed off. He's knocking, but He's not going to break the door down. You have to open it.

And when you do, He's not just promising to clean things up – He's offering life. Real life.

"I have come that they may have life, and have it to the full" (John 10:10).

That's the thing about Jesus – He doesn't just unlock the cell and walk away. He takes you by the hand, leads you out, and invites you into something better.

But you've got to let Him. You've got to decide you're done being chained up, done making peace with your prison.

So what's your chain? What's the thing you've been calling "just the way I am" when it's really bondage?

Don't dress it up. Don't explain it away. Name it. And then start knocking until the One who holds the keys swings that door wide open.

Because He will.

Growth

What has you feeling trapped – and what's stopping you from banging on that door until Jesus opens it?

Grace

Jesus doesn't just promise freedom – He paid for it. Let Him in, so He can let you out.

Week 19 — *Surrounded*

"For troubles surround me – too many to count! My sins pile up so high I can't see my way out. They outnumber the hairs on my head. I have lost all courage" (Psalm 40:12 NLT).

"Please, Lord, rescue me! Come quickly, Lord, and help me" (Psalm 40:13 NLT).

"You are my helper and my savior. O my God, do not delay" (Psalm 40:17b NLT).

Have you ever been completely surrounded by mountains? Not the postcard kind you admire from a scenic overlook, but the kind that make you feel hemmed in, small, maybe even trapped? I've sat in a meadow in the Smokies and another in the Rockies where I could see no way out – just walls of rock and timber pressing in from every side. And yet, when I stuck to the road, eventually I'd find my way around, over, or through what looked impossible at first glance.

I'll never forget one particular motorcycle trip I took alone through the Rockies from Arizona up into Wyoming. Riding a bike through the mountains is a different animal than driving a car. No steel frame, no air conditioning, no windshield wipers, no roof over your head. You're just exposed. It's raw, vulnerable, and honestly, a little crazy.

On that trip I had to slam on the brakes when an elk herd decided to claim the highway as their own. Later, I ducked under an overhang for cover when golf-ball-sized hail pelted me so hard I thought it would dent my helmet. Snow in June forced me to creep along icy curves on tires barely wide enough for balance. I dodged thunderstorms, lightning strikes, fallen trees, loose rocks, and yes – even a bear that was way too close for comfort. Throw in a dozen near misses with deer, and you can see why I came home both exhausted and grateful.

Mountains have a way of humbling you. They can inspire awe, but they can also scare the life out of you. And most of the time – 99.9 percent of the time – you make it through just fine if you stay on the road. But it's that 0.1 percent possibility of disaster that keeps you on edge.

That trip reminded me, life is a lot like that. Sometimes the "mountains" we face aren't made of granite and snow – they're made of bills, broken relationships, bad news from the doctor, or mistakes we can't take back. And when those troubles surround us, it can feel just as intimidating as sitting in that meadow with mountains pressing in from every side.

David knew that feeling. He prayed, "For troubles surround me – too many to count!... I can't see my way out" (Psalm 40:12). That could've been ripped straight from my own journal. There have been plenty of times when I've prayed almost those exact words. Maybe you have too.

Here's the thing I've had to remind myself, it's not weakness to admit you're surrounded. It's not failure to feel vulnerable. It's human. David himself – king, warrior, giant-slayer – cried out, "Please, Lord, rescue me! Come quickly, Lord, and help me" (Psalm 40:13 NLT). That's not a resignation speech – that's faith in the middle of fear.

I'll be honest, I don't like feeling weak. I don't like admitting I can't handle something. But every time I've reached that point – back against the wall, mountains closing in – I've found God to be faithful. Not always in the way I expected, and rarely on my timeline, but never absent.

It's okay to feel surrounded. Just don't camp there. Call out. Pray. Hand it over. As David ended that same psalm, "You are my helper and my savior. O my God, do not delay" (Psalm 40:17 NLT).

That's the kind of prayer that cuts through the mountains.

Growth

What "mountains" are surrounding you right now, and have you stopped to cry out to God for direction – or are you still trying to muscle your own way through?

Grace

When you're surrounded and overwhelmed, don't panic – pray. God knows the way out, even when you don't.

Week 20 —
You Will Surely Die

"Today I have given you the choice between life and death, between blessings and curses... Oh, that you would choose life... You can make this choice by loving the Lord your God, obeying him, and committing yourself firmly to him. This is the key to your life" (Deuteronomy 30:19–20 NLT).

"The thing is to understand myself, to see what God really wishes me to do; the thing is to find a truth which is true for me, to find the idea for which I can live and die." – Søren Kierkegaard

Birthdays are funny things. As kids, we can't wait for them – cake, presents, a number that makes us feel older and more important. In our teens, we chase them because each one unlocks something new – driver's license, voting, maybe even a drink. By young adulthood, birthdays are an excuse to celebrate with friends, stay out late, and feel like life is just starting. But somewhere along the way, we start flinching when the number goes up. We joke about not adding candles to the cake, about getting over-the-hill. And then, in the later years, birthdays can feel like borrowed time – something we hold onto with both hands.

Time moves fast. Faster than we expect. And nothing makes that more obvious than birthdays.

I own a red t-shirt that captures the reality of time in a way that makes people either laugh – or squirm. Bold white letters stretch across the front, "You will surely die." Nothing else. No explanation. No small print. Just those four blunt words.

I picked it up on a mission trip. It was a nod to my late dear friend, Dr. Donald Gillette, who runs Because We Care Ministries in Nicaragua. Don had a habit of tossing out that phrase whenever someone was doing something careless – like chewing dirty fingernails, walking around barefoot, or leaving food uncovered in a third-world village where parasites and disease can take you out in a heartbeat. "You will surely die," he says, half-joking, half-dead serious.

That shirt has gotten some interesting reactions. One young woman wore hers on the flight home, and TSA wasn't nearly as amused as Don. She made it through security, but after enough sideways looks and whispered concerns from fellow passengers, we gently suggested she cover it up.

Here's the kicker though, Don didn't come up with the line. God did. In Genesis 2:17 (ESV), God told Adam plainly, "You may surely eat of every tree… but of the tree of the knowledge of good and evil you shall not eat, for in the day that you eat of it you shall surely die."

Adam disobeyed. And from that moment forward, death has been part of our story. The brokenness, the sickness, the grief – it all traces back to that choice. Every birthday we celebrate is another reminder, we're not getting younger. "You will surely die" isn't just a slogan on a shirt – it's reality.

But here's the better news, God didn't leave it there. Where Adam's choice brought death, Jesus' choice brought life. Paul explains it this way in Romans 5, "Adam's sin led to condemnation, but God's free gift leads to our being made right with God… even though we are guilty of many sins. But even greater is God's wonderful grace… for all who receive it will live in triumph over sin and death."

That's the real choice. Not whether you'll grow older, or whether you'll eventually die – we don't get a say in that. The choice is what you'll do with the days you've got left.

A friend of mine used to grin at me and say, "I'm not dead yet!" It was his way of poking fun at age and illness, but also of reminding himself, if I'm still here, God's still got something for me to do. That line always stuck with me.

And it connects right back to Deuteronomy 30, God sets before us life and death, blessings and curses. Then He pleads, "Choose life." Not just existence. Not just checking birthdays off the calendar. Real life. Life aligned with Him – loving Him, obeying Him, walking with Him.

That's the key to your life. Not money. Not accomplishments. Not even the number of candles on your cake. The key is whether you've chosen the Giver of life Himself.

Growth

What choices are you making with your time and energy – and are they aligned with what God is calling you to do?

Grace

You still have a choice. Choose life. Choose God. That is the key to your life.

Week 21 —
Off Track

"Your word is a lamp to my feet and a light for my path" (Psalm 119:105).

"But when he, the Spirit of truth, comes, he will guide you into all truth" (John 16:13).

"What do we do now?" she asked.

We sat there in silence, staring out the windshield, not quite believing what had just happened. The GPS had led us exactly where it said it would – but here we were, in the wrong city on the wrong day for the concert. Everything about the plan had felt right. Every turn we took seemed to confirm that we were on track. Until suddenly, we weren't.

Her question hung in the air louder than she realized, especially for a guy who thought he was in control. *What do we do now?*

It reminded me of another time I had trusted a GPS. I had just bought my very first unit – a fancy gadget back then – and a group of us guys from church were riding a bus to a conference in South Carolina. I proudly mounted it on the dash and let it lead us. Sure enough, it took us safely through rest stops, hotel searches, and meal breaks. Everyone was impressed. One older gentleman especially kept asking question after question about how it worked, fascinated by this little box that could tell us exactly where to go.

During a lull in the chatter, I half-joked, "Wouldn't it be awesome to have something like this in your brain for life's choices – something that guided you through decisions, detours, and dangers?"

Everyone on the bus laughed, but just then, something stirred in me. It wasn't a joke anymore. Deep inside, I felt the gentle nudge of a familiar truth, "My sheep know my voice" (John 10:27 CEV).

That voice wasn't mine. It was His.

I've never raised sheep, but I use to raise mallard ducks. I brought them home from the feed store when they were tiny puffballs, barely bigger than my hand. I fed them, cared for them, and protected them. As they grew, I moved them out to the pond, where they learned to swim, fly and fend for themselves. They could have left, but they didn't.

In the winter, I'd call to them across the frozen pond. At first, they'd hesitate, cautious. But the moment they heard my voice, they came waddling as fast as their little legs could carry them – quacking, beeping, chattering the whole way. My wife pointed out that they only came when I called. Anyone else, and they would scatter or take flight. They didn't trust every voice. Just mine.

That's the point. In life, we all follow the voice we know and trust.

The concert mix-up? It happened because we listened to the wrong voice that told us who, what, when, and where. And the GPS wasn't malicious – it was well-intentioned. It wasn't wrong, we just didn't double-check our who, what, and where. We just followed along, blind and unquestioning, until we ended up in the wrong place.

And that's how a lot of people live. Trusting someone else's directions. Assuming the crowd must know the way. Floating along on good intentions, but never really checking the source.

I once read a tragic story about three teenage girls in Florida. They were struck and killed while hanging out on a railroad trestle. The responders said they had options. Just a few feet away was another track they could have jumped over to. Below them was a river – deep, slow-moving, survivable if they had jumped. But they didn't move. Fear, indecision, disbelief – it locked them in place. And it cost them everything.

That story haunts me because spiritually, the same thing happens all the time. People freeze. They drift along on the wrong track. They trust the wrong voice. They assume they've got time, more chances, more room to maneuver. But when danger comes, they don't move.

Here's the good news, God hasn't left us to guess the way. He has given us His Word as a light to our feet and His Spirit as a guide into all truth. His voice is trustworthy, even when all other voices are confusing or misleading. When you learn to recognize that voice – through Scripture, through prayer, through the quiet leading of the Spirit – you will know the way.

Don't wait until there's danger to realize you're on the wrong track. Don't follow the crowd, feelings, or even good intentions if they're not rooted in truth. Stop and listen. Tune your ear to the Good Shepherd's voice. His path doesn't just keep you safe – it leads you to life.

Growth

Whose voice are you trusting to guide your life right now? If you've found yourself off track, what would it look like to change course and follow God's voice instead?

Grace

Don't wait until it's too late to realize you're on the wrong track. Listen for the voice you can trust – God's. It will always lead you toward life.

Week 22 — *Breathing Lessons*

"Then Jesus said to him, 'Get up! Pick up your mat and walk'" (John 5:8).

I'd been sitting in my hunting blind for about two hours. It was one of those cold, crisp December mornings in the Virginia mountains – the kind where every sound carries, and every breath feels sacred. The kind of morning that makes you thankful to be alive, whether you bag a deer or not.

I leaned over to check the right-side window. It didn't have as clear a view as the front or the left, but I'd occasionally scan it just in case something moved out there on the trail. That's when it happened.

A warm, gentle breeze brushed across my face. It felt almost like the soft brush of a kiss from the mountain itself – unexpected, peaceful, and oddly intimate. I froze. Took a slow, deep breath. And thought:

There's just no good substitute for breathing.

Now, if you've never had to think about your breathing, you might not understand that moment. But I've had asthma since I was a kid. Breathing, for me, has never been something I could take for granted. I've had times when every breath felt like a battle – when my chest tightened, air wouldn't come, and panic rose faster than my lungs could keep up.

That's part of the reason I run. It's not because I'm obsessed with exercise, though most days I enjoy it. I run because it keeps my lungs strong. It keeps me in the fight. No shortcuts. Running costs me something, but it gives me something too, strength, stamina, and breath.

And if I'm honest? I think life with God is a lot like that.

We want healing, but not the discipline that helps us stay whole. We want peace, but without the stillness it requires. We want to move forward, but we'd rather someone else do the walking.

But God's invitation isn't passive. It's active.

I think about the man at the pool of Bethesda. He'd been lying there, stuck, waiting for thirty-eight years. Almost four decades of "maybe tomorrow." Jesus walked up to him and asked a question that sounds ridiculous at first, "Do you want to get well?" (John 5:6 NLT).

Of course he wanted to get well – or did he? Because Jesus didn't offer to carry him or magically change the water. He gave the man a command, "Get up! Pick up your mat and walk."

The healing was there. The miracle was available. But the man had to respond.

And that's how God still works. He's not looking for perfection. He's looking for participation. He wants you to breathe. To rise. To move.

Maybe for you, it's not asthma. Maybe it's addiction. Or anger. Or apathy. Maybe it's doubt, debt, depression, or grief. Maybe you're spiritually winded and don't know how to catch your breath again. You've been lying in the same spot for so long it's starting to feel like home.

But God is still speaking. He still breathes life. And He's still saying, "Get up."

Sometimes the hardest part of faith is the first inhale. The first step. The decision to stop waiting for someone else to fix it and instead trust God enough to move.

So try this with me right now. Close your eyes. Take a slow, deep breath. Let it out. As you exhale, imagine releasing your worry, frustration, and fear. Then inhale again, and with that breath whisper a prayer, "Lord, help me to stand. Help me to walk."

You may not be able to fix everything today. But you can take one step. And no one can take that step for you.

Growth

What's something you've been waiting on God to fix that He may be asking you to take a step toward instead? Where do you need to breathe, rise, and walk?

Grace

There's no substitute for standing up and doing the thing that needs to be done. God will meet you – but He often waits for you to move first. So take a breath and begin.

Week 23 —
The Sacred Paradigm Shift

"This is how we know what love is, Jesus Christ laid down his life for us. And we ought to lay down our lives for our brothers and sisters... Dear children, let us not love with words or speech but with actions and in truth" (1 John 3:16–18).

We didn't walk into the hospital chapel to pray – not at first. We were just looking for a break from the sterile smell of alcohol and disinfectant, the endless beeping of machines, and the haunting rise and fall of the monitors in the ICU. She was dying – too young, too kind, too full of love for it to make sense. We were exhausted and hollow, wandering the halls like people without a map.

And then, like stumbling on a hidden doorway in the middle of a storm, we found the chapel. A quiet space tucked just steps away from the chaos. We slipped inside and sat down, grateful for a moment to breathe.

At first, no one prayed. We whispered, we cried, we stared at the floor. But slowly, the urge to pray bubbled up – not because we had great hope of healing, but because our souls couldn't carry the grief alone. We prayed for comfort. For clarity. Maybe just to feel something besides despair.

That's when it happened.

The lights didn't dim, but the room seemed to soften. The air felt different – warm, almost holy. And then I heard it. Not with my ears, but deep inside:

"This is not about you."

The words shook me. It felt like being undone and rebuilt at the same time. I opened my eyes and realized I was no longer sitting – I'd wandered toward a stained-glass window, staring through it like I expected to see beyond the glass. And when we all began to share, it turned out every single one of us had "heard" the same thing:

"This is not about you."

We didn't fully understand it, but somehow the words brought peace.

Years later, I'm still unpacking that moment. And the truth is simple, but not shallow, most of us live as if everything revolves around us. Our grief, our comfort, our desires, our need for answers. But in that sacred whisper, God was gently shifting our perspective.

It didn't mean our pain didn't matter – because it did. He saw it. He carried it with us. But the story of redemption was never meant to circle only around us. It's bigger. Wider. It's about all of us. And it's about those who haven't yet heard or experienced His love.

That's what love does, it pulls us out of ourselves and moves us toward others.

And this love isn't fragile. It's not just a feeling or a fleeting sentiment. It's eternal. It's what carried Jesus to the cross, and it's what calls us to love with more than words – love with action, with sacrifice, with truth.

So yes, you hurt. Yes, you carry grief. Yes, sometimes it feels unbearable. But if you've received the kind of love that heals and restores, then it's not just for you. It's meant to flow through you. Beyond the tears. Beyond the pain. Into a world desperate for hope.

Growth

Where in your life are you still living as if it's all about you? What step can you take today to let God's love flow through you – beyond words, into action?

Grace

The love of God was never meant to stop with you. Let it move you past your pain and into purpose. Don't just feel it – live it.

Week 24 —
What For?

"Their people, drained of power, are dismayed and put to shame.

They are like plants in the field, like tender green shoots,

like grass sprouting on the roof, scorched before it grows up" (Isaiah 37:27).

She's exhausted, but not tired. Cold, but somehow not feeling cold.

Her lips are chapped and cracked, her skin raw from saltwater. Her ears are inflamed, her tongue is swollen, and her limbs feel foreign – kicking on their own. And yet, deep inside, there's a core of warmth – embers glowing under the surface, refusing to go out.

Gertrude "Trudy" Ederle had already made a name for herself with the Women's Swimming Association. The pool wasn't her only stage – she thrived in the open water. After winning gold at the 1924 Olympics, she set her sights on the English Channel.

Her first attempt in 1925 ended in illness and disappointment. Most would have stopped there. But Trudy wasn't most people.

On her second try, she faced wind, rain, and fog for 14.5 hours straight. At one point, the storm got so bad her support crew lost sight of her and panicked.

They shouted from the boat, "Come on out, girl!"

She looked up, smiled, and shouted back, "What for?"

That's not the answer of a victim. That's the answer of someone who's already decided she's going to the other side.

So what makes a person keep going when everything says stop?

What transforms a victim into the victorious?

Consider Joshua. Forty years in the wilderness. Moses – his mentor and leader – was gone. The promised land was still ahead, but so were fortified cities and enemy armies. God's instructions weren't just a pep talk – they were declarations meant to shape Joshua's identity:

"No one will be able to stand against you all the days of your life.

As I was with Moses, so I will be with you; I will never leave you nor forsake you.

Be strong and courageous... Have I not commanded you? Be strong and courageous.

Do not be terrified; do not be discouraged, for the LORD your God will be with you wherever you go" (Joshua 1:5–9).

God knew Joshua would face fear and discouragement – so He addressed them head-on.

Peter adds another layer to the warning:

"Be self-controlled and alert. Your enemy the devil prowls around like a roaring lion looking for someone to devour" (1 Peter 5:8).

And here's the thing – Satan's primary weapon isn't claws or teeth. It's discouragement. To be disheartened is to have your courage, hope, or enthusiasm drained away. That's how he hunts – by making you believe you've already lost.

But the truth?

Your soul is safe in the arms of Christ – even when the storm wins against your body.

So don't run. Don't give in. Don't hand your victory away before the fight is over.

James tells us:

"Come near to God and he will come near to you" (James 4:8).

Draw close. Let Him take the storm that was meant to sink you and turn it into the very thing that builds you. Let Him make you more than a survivor – let Him make you victorious.

If you're tempted to quit, remember Trudy in the middle of the English Channel, smiling through wind and waves and saying, "What for?"

That's what courage sounds like when you know God is with you in the middle of it.

Growth

Where have you been tempted to quit – and what would change if you believed that God was with you in the middle of it?

Grace

You're not a victim of your circumstances. You're a child of God – and He's already declared you victorious.

Stage 4

Perseverance Under Pressure

Week 25 —
Seven Long Days

"Why am I discouraged? Why is my heart so sad? I will put my hope in God! I will praise him again – my Savior and my God" (Psalm 42:11).

My doctor gave me *that look*. You know the one. Eyebrows raised, head tilted, disappointment written all over his face. "You're almost sixty and you still haven't had a colonoscopy?"

I didn't bother explaining that my previous two doctors had said the same thing. Truth is, I'd been dragging my feet for years. Pride, maybe. Fear, definitely. And if I'm honest? Deep down, I didn't really want to know what was going on inside me.

Cancer runs through my family like an uninvited guest who never leaves. We don't even like saying the word – we call it "The Big C." It's taken too many of us, my mom, my sister, my Mamaw and Papaw, and several aunts and uncles. So no, I wasn't exactly sprinting toward the possibility of adding my name to that list.

Still, I finally said yes. The prep was brutal. Twenty-four hours of nothing but liquid. Twelve hours of flushing everything out of my system. Somewhere around hour ten, I thought, *this has to be worse than whatever they might find.*

The actual procedure? A breeze. No pain, just a little embarrassment. I got dressed, waited for the doctor, and expected the usual, "All clear. See you in ten years."

But that's not what I got.

"We found one small polyp. Probably nothing to worry about. We'll send it off to pathology and call you in about a week."

A week? Just like that, I was dropped into no-man's land. Stuck in the waiting. Stuck in the fear. Stuck in the what-ifs. What if I'm next? What if this is the start of the story that I've seen unfold too many times before?

Normally, I'm not a worrier. I lean toward optimism, faith, and facing things head-on. But fear has a way of slipping through the cracks. Those seven days felt like seven years. Every random ache turned suspicious. Every thought wandered down dark alleys. And the worst part? I couldn't do a thing about it. Just wait.

Day seven finally came. The letter arrived. My hands shook as I tore it open. I skimmed past all the medical jargon until my eyes locked onto the words I'd been desperate to see:

"Totally benign and of no significance."

I exhaled. Deep. The kind of breath you don't even realize you've been holding until it finally breaks free.

And then it hit me, I'd let fear steal seven days of my life. Seven days of peace, sleep, and joy – all wasted on scenarios that never happened. Fear hadn't changed a single thing about the outcome. All it did was rob me of the present.

Scripture says "Fear not" or some version of it 365 times. Once for every single day of the year. That's not coincidence. That's God saying, *I know how easily fear grabs you. But trust Me instead. I've got you.*

Psalm 42 captures that tension perfectly – the heaviness of despair battling against the stubbornness of hope. Even when we don't know the outcome, we can still praise. Even in the waiting, we can lean into the One who holds the final word.

Growth

Is fear quietly shaping the way you think, decide, or live? What would it look like to turn that fear into trust – one day at a time?

Grace

Fear doesn't fix a thing. But faith anchors you while you wait. Whatever report you're dreading, whatever weight you're carrying – put your hope in God. He is your peace, even across seven long days.

Week 26 —
Where Is God?

"So let God work his will in you. Yell a loud no to the devil and watch him scamper. Say a quiet yes to God and he'll be there in no time… Get down on your knees before the Master; it's the only way you'll get on your feet" (James 4:7–10 The Message).

Where is God?

It's not a churchy question – it's a gut-level one. Especially when the headlines scream war, kids are gunned down in schools, families are splintered, and people you love get crushed under the weight of life. Even in our own homes, heartache can knock the breath out of us. And in those moments, the question rises whether we say it out loud or not, *Where are you, God?*

I've asked it. Not politely. Not with bowed head and folded hands. But with frustration, fists clenched, and voice raised, *Why don't you do more? Why do you let this stuff happen?*

And here's the shocker – I got an answer. Not an explanation. Not a theological lecture. Just peace. Like a sudden calm in the middle of a storm. And then came the whisper, sharp and cutting, *This isn't Me. This is you.*

James 4 puts it plainly:

"Where do you think all these appalling wars and quarrels come from?

Do you think they just happen? Think again. They come about because you want your own way, and fight for it deep inside yourselves..."

That stings. Because it's true. The evil we blame on God is usually born in human hearts – greed, pride, lust for power, selfishness. We want our way, and when we don't get it, we fight. Nations fight. Families fight. Churches fight. And the fallout looks a lot like the mess we see all around us.

But James doesn't just throw shade – he points to the way out:

"What he gives in love is far better than anything else you'll find. So let God work his will in you."

Translation? Stop blaming. Start surrendering. Stop asking where God is – while shoving Him out of your life. He's right here. He's always been here. But He doesn't kick the door down. He waits for an honest yes.

And when you give Him that yes? He doesn't just show up – He moves in. He strengthens. He restores. He takes your cracked, broken, messy life and breathes hope into it.

So, where is God? Not missing. Not absent. Not asleep. He's waiting for you to drop the act, take a knee, and invite Him in.

Growth

Where in your life are you blaming God for what's really the result of your own way – or the world's way? What would it look like to stop running and finally say yes to Him?

Grace

God isn't the problem. He's the answer. But you'll only find Him when you stop fighting for your way and surrender to His.

Week 27 —
Words to Live By

"Blessed is the one who perseveres under trial because, having stood the test, that person will receive the crown of life that the Lord has promised to those who love him" (James 1:12).

It's no secret that my dad and I didn't exactly get along when I was a kid. Between his temper and my rebellious streak, we were a bad match – like oil and water, or maybe gasoline and a match. Still, we shared some common ground.

We both loved football. We both loved hunting – though strangely, never together. We both loved fast cars and long road trips. And we both liked fixing things.

My dad was a skilled tool-and-die machinist who also ran a busy side gig as a mechanic. At any given time, there could be fifteen or twenty cars lined up in our driveway, waiting on his hands. From him, I inherited a knack for tools. But when it came to working together? Forget it. Our projects usually ended in more shouting than progress.

So I tinkered on my own. Old radios, lawnmowers, whatever I could get my hands on – I tore them apart just to see how they worked. Sometimes I even got them put back together with only a few mystery pieces left over. Success.

But my real teacher wasn't my dad. It was our elderly neighbor, Mr. Sewell – "Mr. S." I never knew his first name. He just lived across the street, two doors down, and for reasons I never understood, he took a liking to me.

He taught me how to fish, how to garden, how to work hard. The jobs my dad had to threaten me into doing, I'd gladly do for Mr. S. He was patient and steady, never raising his voice, never giving up on a project – or on me. Hot days, greasy hands, busted knuckles – I didn't mind. I just wanted to be around him. Kids can tell when someone truly sees them, truly likes them.

Together, we became the neighborhood's unofficial "shade-tree mechanics," fixing lawnmowers, chainsaws, trimmers – whatever people brought over. I didn't just learn about engines. I learned perseverance and tenacity.

One day he told me he was moving to Florida. I was crushed. On his last day, he handed me ten of his handmade bamboo fishing poles, gave me a big bear hug (the first I remember from him), and said a few simple words I'll never forget:

"The difference between people isn't always talent or education. Mostly, Lar, it's just plain stick-to-it-ness."

That phrase – stick-to-it-ness – got under my skin in the best way. A year later, when I learned he had passed away, I went to the basement and pulled out those bamboo poles. I sat there thinking about him – not the engines or the fish, but the way he listened, the way he believed in me, and those words he left behind.

Stick-to-it-ness. Perseverance. The kind of grit James wrote about when he said those who "stand the test" will receive the crown of life.

Mr. S. lived it. And by God's grace, I want to live it too. Those words weren't just advice. They became words to live by.

Growth

Who has modeled perseverance for you? And where do you need a little more "stick-to-it-ness" in your own life today?

Grace

Perseverance may not be flashy, but it will take you further than talent ever will. Sometimes the greatest words to live by are the ones spoken quietly by someone who simply shows up and sticks with you.

Week 28 —
This is Not a Spectator Sport

"...From him the whole body, joined and held together by every supporting ligament, grows and builds itself up in love, as each part does its work" (Ephesians 4:16).

I'm not joking – you really can pay someone to exercise for you.

Hand over your money, and somebody out there will gladly run the miles, do the push-ups, and lift the weights while you sit on the couch. But here's the reality, when life hits and strength is required – carrying groceries, shoveling snow, running to help someone, or fighting for your own health – you won't have it. They will. Their body will be stronger. Yours won't.

And everyone knows this truth, you can't outsource your workouts. If you want strength, you have to sweat for it yourself.

So why do we think our spiritual lives work any differently?

Too many of us try to contract out our faith. We want the pastor to know the Bible, the worship leader to experience the Spirit, the prayer team to cry out for God's power. We sit back like spectators – then wonder why, when temptation comes or suffering blindsides us, we crumble.

The apostle Paul was blunt about this. In Ephesians 4, he said church leaders aren't there to do your faith for you – they're there to equip you. To train you. To prepare you so that you grow into maturity and strength. That means one thing, you've got to do the reps yourself.

Read the Word. Pray out loud. Worship even when it feels awkward. Fast when it costs you something. Practice spiritual disciplines the same way an athlete trains – consistently, intentionally, with eyes on the prize.

And here's the best part, just like working out, you don't have to do it alone. Anybody who's ever tried to train by themselves knows how easy it is to skip, quit, or coast. But with a team? With a coach? With a friend? You push harder. You go farther. You show up because someone else is counting on you.

That's what the church is supposed to be. Not a place to outsource your faith, but a gym for the soul. A training ground where we push each other, encourage each other, and grow together until we look more like Jesus.

So stop paying other people to sweat for you. Stop admiring someone else's spiritual muscle while yours atrophies. Pick up your Bible. Bend your knees. Join your voice with the body of Christ. Train your soul – and do it together.

Growth

Are you sitting back while others work out spiritually on your behalf? What one habit can you start – or restart – this week to strengthen your own walk with God?

Grace

You can't hire out your faith. Spiritual strength is built the same way as physical strength, through training, perseverance, and showing up.

Week 29 —
God and Power Tools

"He gives strength to the weary and increases the power of the weak...
but those who hope in the Lord will renew their strength.

They will soar on wings like eagles; they will run and not grow weary,
they will walk and not be faint" (Isaiah 40:29, 31).

I have some hedges in front of my house. A lot of hedges. If you've
ever had to maintain hedges, you know – unless your best friend is
Edward Scissorhands – you need a good hedge trimmer.

Twice a year, I break mine out, once in late spring, and again in the
fall. This keeps the yard tidy and the path to the front door visible.
But my story isn't really about the hedges – it's about the trimmer.

When I first bought my hedge trimmer, I was excited. It wasn't just
any model – it was a top-of-the-line cordless powerhouse. No more
dragging extension cords through bushes or worrying about where to
plug in. This was freedom. This was efficiency. This was the tool that
would turn me into a "hedgertist." (Yes, that's my own word.)

As I started shaping, curving, and carving my bushes with artistic
flair, I felt like a suburban Michelangelo. Grinning from ear to ear, I
imagined the neighbors admiring my "bushelicious botanicals."

And then, it died. The trimmer that is.

Just like that, my glorious trimmer – my symbol of yard domination – went completely silent. Battery dead.

Five hours later, it was charged and ready. I returned to battle, motivation slightly diminished. Thirty minutes later, it quit again. And again. And again.

That's when it hit me. Power tools are only useful if they actually have power. The same is true for chainsaws, vacuums, drills, weed eaters – you name it. Without power, they're just expensive paperweights.

It's the same for people.

The Bible says:

"Their people, drained of power, are dismayed and put to shame. They are like plants in the field, like tender green shoots, like grass sprouting on the roof, scorched even before it grows up" (Isaiah 37:27).

Ever felt like that? Drained? Burned out before you even get going?

If we're honest, most of us have. We try to power through life on our own strength – facing challenges, heartbreak, disappointment, and temptation – all while slowly losing the charge we once had. And just like that hedge trimmer, we shut down. Spiritually, emotionally, sometimes even physically.

But here's the good news, we were never meant to power ourselves.

Just as our physical bodies need fuel, our spirits need a source of energy too. And the Bible tells us what that source is, the Holy Spirit. It's not just religious language – it's spiritual reality. We were made to operate best when we're plugged into the One who made us.

Colossians 1:18 says,

"And he is the head of the body, the church; he is the beginning and the firstborn from among the dead, so that in everything he might have the supremacy."

In other words, Jesus isn't just a part of our story – He's the power source for the entire system. When we try to do life apart from Him, it's no wonder we lose energy. It's no wonder we struggle.

But when we stay connected?

Isaiah 40 says:

"He gives strength to the weary... those who hope in the Lord will renew their strength. They will soar... they will run and not grow weary, they will walk and not faint."

That's not poetry. That's a promise.

So if you're feeling weak, weary, or completely spent – don't beat yourself up. Don't panic. Just check the power source. Have you been running on your own strength? Or are you plugged in?

Growth

Where have you been running on empty? What would it look like for you to recharge – not with more rest or distraction – but by reconnecting with God?

Grace

Power tools are only as useful as their connection to power. So are we. Stay connected to the source, and you'll be charged with strength that never runs dry.

Week 30 —
You're Not Finished

"...in all things God works for the good of those who love him, who have been called according to his purpose" (Romans 8:28).

Do you get discouraged? Yeah, me too.

I couldn't tell you exactly when I got so discouraged – or even why. It started like a dull headache and slowly built until I couldn't ignore it. Eventually, I found myself asking, *What the heck is wrong with me?*

It's an honest question. I have a great life – wonderful wife, grown kids I'm proud of, an adorable grandson, and work I enjoy. I have enough time to focus on what matters most. Who wouldn't be grateful for that?

You might say I was just pouting or ungrateful. Maybe I was. But this time felt different. It wasn't just about me – I was discouraged for others.

See, I'm driven to help people. It's wired into who I am. But lately, I've felt like my efforts haven't made much of a dent. Like everything I pour out disappears into a black hole. No visible results. No transformation. Just noise in the chaos.

Then, during a conversation with a few trusted guys I hang out with, the fog began to lift. As we talked, I realized what had been gnawing at me wasn't just current disappointment – it was regret. Regret over how many times I've messed up in the past. Regret that I might've hurt people instead of helped them. Regret that my selfishness "back then" may be limiting my impact now.

And that hit me hard. Because right now, the world is hurting. The people I care about are hurting. There's so much hate, fear, sickness, loss, anger, and apathy – it's overwhelming. And I keep wondering, *What if I'm the reason some people doubt God even exists?*

How do you offer hope when you've been part of the problem?

That's when one of my guys gently reminded me, "God doesn't need you to be perfect to use you." He's not weak because we are. In fact, His power is often clearest when we finally get out of the way.

Romans 8:28 came to mind:

"…in all things God works for the good of those who love him…"

Notice it doesn't say *all things are good*. Because let's be real – some things in life truly stink. But God? He works *good out of the bad* for those who love Him.

That's where grace comes in.

It doesn't erase what's been done. But it rewrites what can happen next. It makes room for healing, growth, and redemption. Even when we've made a mess of things, God can still use us – not just despite our past, but because of it.

James 1:5 says,

"If you don't know what you're doing, pray to the Father. He loves to help" (MSG).

That's the answer to my discouragement. Not trying harder. Not carrying guilt. Not wallowing. Just going to God – honestly – and asking for help. Again.

Philippians 4:6–7 ties it all together:

"Do not be anxious about anything, but in every situation, by prayer and petition, with thanksgiving, present your requests to God.

And the peace of God, which transcends all understanding, will guard your hearts and your minds in Christ Jesus."

That's the kind of peace I needed. That's the kind of peace I'm learning to rest in again.

So today, if you're feeling discouraged – whether by your own shortcomings or the weight of the world – don't give up. Don't spiral. And please don't believe the lie that your past disqualifies you from making a difference.

You're not finished. And God's not done.

Growth

Have you been letting regret or discouragement hold you back from helping others? What would it look like to surrender that to God – and trust Him to work good out of it?

Grace

God isn't limited by your past. He can redeem your mistakes and bring beauty from your brokenness – if you'll give it to Him.

Week 31 —
God Doesn't Waste Dirt

"The LORD is my shepherd, I shall not be in want. He makes me lie down in green pastures, he leads me beside quiet waters, he restores my soul" (Psalm 23:1–3).

Help. It's a simple word – but when your soul is the one crying it out, it's anything but simple. You've probably heard the phrase, "Help, I've fallen, and I can't get up." It started as a cheesy infomercial, but let's be honest – it hits different when it's your spirit gasping it in the dark.

There's an old story about a farmer's donkey that fell into a dry well. The animal cried for hours as the farmer considered his options. The well was useless. The donkey was old. Finally, the farmer decided to bury it. He called his neighbors, and together they began shoveling dirt into the well.

At first, the donkey panicked, braying in fear. But then something shifted. With each shovel of dirt, the animal shook it off and stepped up. Shovel by shovel, the pit that was meant to end him became the very thing that raised him. Eventually, he stepped over the rim and walked away.

That picture hit me hard this week – because lately, I've felt like that donkey. Trapped in a pit I dug myself. Expecting joy and peace but winding up with exhaustion and emptiness instead. Not because life ambushed me – but because I stopped trusting God and tried to dig my own way. Now? I feel stuck, buried under regret, shame, and fear.

Ever been there? Maybe you're there right now. The pit feels deep. The dirt keeps coming. And hope feels like it belongs to somebody else.

But here's what I'm learning, God doesn't waste dirt. What the enemy means to bury you, God can use to raise you. Every pile of regret, fear, or failure can become a step closer to Him – if you'll let Him. That's grace. That's redemption.

Psalm 38 gives voice to this kind of despair:

"My guilt has overwhelmed me like a burden too heavy to bear... I wait for you, O LORD; you will answer, O Lord my God."

That's the cry of a soul in the well. But Psalm 23 gives the answer, "He restores my soul. He leads me beside quiet waters."

God doesn't just throw you a ladder – He climbs down into the pit with you. He restores what you thought was lost. He whispers hope. He reminds you you're not forgotten. And then, one shovel at a time, He lifts you out.

So if you're overwhelmed, stuck, or too tired to climb – don't give up. Cry out. Shake it off. Step up. And let God turn the dirt into something that lifts you closer to Him.

Growth

What's been weighing you down lately? What would it look like to invite God into the pit instead of trying to climb out alone?

Grace

When you feel buried, remember, God doesn't waste dirt. What was meant to break you, He can use to raise you.

Week 32 —
Field of Dreams

"And the seeds that fell on the good soil represent honest, good-hearted people who hear God's word, cling to it, and patiently produce a huge harvest" (Luke 8:15 NLT).

My momma loved her garden. To her, a home-grown vegetable was a true treasure. Unfortunately, she rarely had the time to tend to it. Long shifts on her feet as a nurse at the state hospital, followed by caring for a trio of spoiled kids – and their equally spoiled father – left her with little energy for much else.

That's where I came in.

Without any real planning or fanfare, my yearly gift to my momma became the labor of love I poured into that garden plot behind our little suburban home. Every spring, I'd borrow the neighbor's rumbling old rototiller and begin the ritual. The smell of freshly turned earth would rise up in waves, earthy and promising. After tilling, I'd walk the rows with a bow rake, breaking up the clods until we had a smooth, ready soil bed – about twelve by twenty feet. Then came the manure, mixed in until the ground was rich and welcoming, eager for tomato, potato, carrot, green bean, and my personal favorite, watermelon. We'd even line the garden with bright orange marigolds to keep the rabbits at bay.

It was hard work for a young boy, but I was fascinated by the "miracle in the seed," as Momma called it. She'd hold a tiny seed in her palm and say, "There's a whole harvest in here if you just give it time." And most years, I tackled that garden with heart. Most years.

Baseball was my big distraction. Like my older brother before me, I was utterly obsessed with that stitched white hardball. We played everywhere – on our street, in empty lots, cow pastures, little league fields, and in our own yard, where the short chain-link fence turned every would-be home run into an automatic out. I watched games, listened to them on the radio, and collected "priceless" baseball cards featuring my heroes. The boys of summer – especially The Big Red Machine of the '70s from nearby Cincinnati – were my beautiful obsession.

And the cost of that obsession? Well, it was Momma's garden that paid the price.

As much as I loved planting and watching things grow, the slow pace of gardening couldn't quite compete with the excitement of baseball. Each spring I began with the best intentions – wanting her garden to burst with life and make her proud – but to an outsider, it probably looked like I just loved baseball a little bit more. After a strong, enthusiastic start, the garden often succumbed to weeds and neglect by midsummer, producing only a fraction of what it could have. My passion for baseball, on the other hand, thrived.

For a time, it even looked like I might earn a scholarship – maybe even go pro. But a rare and severe case of shingles in my early teens changed everything. The nerve damage to my pitching shoulder ended that dream almost overnight. Crushed, I never returned to the ballfield – or to my momma's garden. What followed were some dark, wandering years. I lost a sense of direction, unsure what field – literal or figurative – I belonged in.

Eventually, I found purpose again… in a different kind of garden. This time, the seeds were spiritual – friendships that encouraged me, a church community that prayed for me, moments in Scripture that took root in my heart. Like Momma's vegetables, they didn't grow overnight. They needed tending, patience, and sometimes a little pulling of weeds.

Truth be told, I still love the feel of a baseball in my hands. I'll roll one around in my palm, massaging it almost like a caress. My office desk is mostly uncluttered, but there in the right front corner sits a prized possession, a baseball signed by the great Johnny Bench.

And as for the garden? It's been years since I tended more than a few tomato plants, some cucumbers, and a small patch of watermelons. But this spring, once again, the soil is calling to me. It's asking me to put aside fruitless distractions and to return to the joy of watching seeds become fruit – slowly, steadily, wonderfully. It feels a little like stepping back onto a familiar ballfield, glove in hand, ready to play again – not for trophies, but for the pure love of the game.

I know my momma is smiling down on me, just like she used to.

"There's a miracle in the seed," she'd say. "A miracle in the seed."

Years later, I have to wonder – was Momma talking about the vegetables, the garden, or something else entirely? Either way, I've learned that in both gardening and faith, you don't win the season in one swing – you win it by showing up, tending carefully, and letting God bring the harvest in His time.

Growth

In life, some seasons feel like baseball – fast, thrilling, full of big plays. Others are like gardening – slow, steady, and quietly growing something that matters. Which season are you in right now, and how are you tending the "field" God has placed you in?

Grace

Seeds only produce a harvest if we care for them faithfully – and the most important ones may not be planted in soil at all.

Stage 5

Perseverance Under Pressure

Week 33 —
A Dollar an Hour

"Whatever you do, work at it with all your heart, as working for the Lord, not for human masters" (Colossians 3:23).

My first paying job was on a neighbor's farm for the grand sum of one dollar an hour. The work wasn't glamorous – tilling soil, planting crops, pulling weeds (and then pulling more weeds), and eventually harvesting whatever survived the bugs, the weather, and my inexperience.

It wasn't much of a paycheck, but the lessons were priceless. That farm was my first classroom in responsibility, perseverance, and the satisfaction of seeing hard work pay off. Sometimes the reward wasn't the harvest at all, but the farmer's quiet nod of appreciation.

Those long, hot days taught me truths no schoolbook ever could, that honest work has value, that effort matters even when no one is watching, and that joy often shows up in simple things like dirt under your fingernails and a job done right.

But here's the twist, as I got older, I wandered from those lessons. I chased paychecks and promotions, climbing ladders that left me strangely empty at the top. No matter how many digits were on the paycheck, it never filled the hollow spot inside.

That's when the old farm lessons resurfaced. The memory of working with my hands, pouring myself into something bigger than me, reminded me of a deeper truth, success isn't measured in dollars. It's measured in passion, purpose, and people.

That doesn't mean I went back to farming. But I did go back to the essence of it – seeking work that mattered, that aligned with my values, that served people instead of just padding pockets. And slowly, fulfillment began to take root again.

It hasn't been easy. Following your calling never is. There are days of doubt and times when the responsibility feels heavy. But there's also joy that money can't buy – the joy of knowing your effort is making a difference in someone else's life.

Today, I measure wealth not by what I own, but by the smiles I bring, the encouragement I can give, and the impact I leave behind. The older I get, the clearer it is, true success is not a destination. It's not about arriving at some perfect job, house, or status. It's the journey itself – the day-in, day-out faithfulness of working with all your heart, for the Lord and for the people He's placed in your path.

And for me, it all started in a farm field, sweating for a dollar an hour, and unknowingly sowing seeds of a lesson that would last a lifetime.

Growth

What was your first-job lesson? How did it shape your view of work – and does the way you live today reflect what truly matters to you?

Grace

True success isn't measured in dollars – it's found in the purpose, joy, and love you pour into the work God gives you.

Week 34 — *Arms Wide Open*

"Cast all your anxiety on him because he cares for you" (1 Peter 5:7).

My young son screamed as he ran, swatting desperately at the angry hornets that swarmed him. I ran alongside, trying to scoop him up, desperate to protect him from the sudden, violent attack.

It had all started so innocently. We'd taken our usual evening walk to our neighbor's porch – the perfect spot to watch the sun sink over the Blue Ridge Mountains. Most nights, the fading light painted the ridges in shades of blue and gray, with a crimson sky that could take your breath away. But that night was remembered for something else entirely, pain.

By the time we got back home, the swelling had set in. I made makeshift ice packs, gave him Benadryl and children's pain medicine, and sat with him while he cried. Even hours later, as his eyes puffed red and heavy with tears, he whispered, "It still hurts, Daddy. It hurts." I cried, too.

Years later, I was stung myself – only a handful of times, but enough to bring that memory flooding back. I could still see his tear-streaked face, his little arms reaching for me, pleading for help I couldn't fully give.

And that's when it hit me, that's exactly how God invites us to come to Him.

Mark 10:13–16 tells us people brought their children to Jesus, and when the disciples tried to turn them away, Jesus rebuked them. "Let the little children come to me," He said. Then He took them in His arms and blessed them.

That's the picture I see when I remember my son's pain, arms open, a father ready to receive hurting children.

Life has its hornets. Unexpected attacks. Repeated stings. Pain that feels unfair. We can either run from God – or run to Him. And when we run to Him, we don't find a cold shoulder or a distant deity. We find arms open wide, full of compassion.

Jesus made that clear. In John 14:9, He told His disciples, "Anyone who has seen me has seen the Father." You want to know what God is like? Look at Jesus. He healed the sick, fed the hungry, comforted the grieving, blessed children, and gave His life for His friends. That's the heart of the Father – present, loving, self-giving.

So when life stings, don't carry the pain alone. Don't let fear or shame drive you farther from Him. Run toward Him. Cry out, "It hurts, Father!" He already knows. And He already cares.

You may still have a few stings, but you'll also find His presence holding you steady, His love restoring your soul, His comfort carrying you through the night.

Growth

What pain or burden are you carrying right now? Have you tried to handle it alone, or will you run to the Father's open arms today?

Grace

When life stings, run to the One who loves you most – His arms are already open.

Week 35 —
Faith Floats

"Come to me, all you who are weary and burdened, and I will give you rest… you will find rest for your souls. For my yoke is easy and my burden is light" (Mat. 11:28–30).

Most swim instructors will tell you the first skill you need in the water isn't the freestyle stroke or the backstroke – it's learning how to float. And the first step to floating? Believe that you can. The second step? Relax.

Easier said than done. Especially when you're in deep water and your natural instinct is to thrash and fight.

But the science is simple, the human body is mostly water, which means it's designed to float more than to sink. Sure, muscle density and body type can affect buoyancy, but the truth is the same – your body wants to stay up if you'll just let it.

And that's when it hit me, the same principle applies to faith.

Spiritually, the steps are the same. First, believe. Then, relax. Your soul was made to rest in God more than it was made to sink in fear, worry, or doubt. But like in swimming, some of us keep kicking and flailing – working harder than we have to – when what we need most is to trust the One who's already holding us.

So how do you learn? You need an instructor. In the water, it's a swim coach. In life, it's the Holy Spirit. Jesus said,

"...the Holy Spirit, whom the Father will send in my name, will teach you all things and will remind you of everything I have said to you. Peace I leave with you; my peace I give you" (John 14:26–27).

That's the promise, not just survival, but peace. Not just keeping your head above water but learning to move through it with confidence. And Jesus told us how to begin:

"Ask and it will be given to you; seek and you will find; knock and the door will be opened to you... how much more will your Father in heaven give good gifts to those who ask him!" (Matthew 7:7–11).

Faith starts where floating starts – by believing you were made for this and by relaxing into the arms that hold you. From there, God doesn't just teach you how to float; He teaches you to swim, to walk, to run, and finally, to rest.

If you feel like you're drowning right now – overwhelmed, exhausted, unsure of how much longer you can keep going – hear this, you already have what you need to float. You don't have to thrash. You don't have to figure it all out. Believe. Relax. Let Him hold you.

Growth

Where in your life are you thrashing when you could be floating? How can you ask the Spirit to help you trust and rest today?

Grace

The key to staying afloat – both in the pool and in faith – is to believe you can and to rest in the One who carries you.

Week 36 —
Mustard Seed TV

"Truly I tell you, if you have faith as small as a mustard seed, you can say to this mountain, 'Move from here to there,' and it will move. Nothing will be impossible for you" (Matthew 17:20).

Years ago, my mom was in a terrible car accident. The car was totaled, but she seemed to walk away with only bumps, bruises, and a stiff neck. The bruises faded. The stiffness did not. In fact, it got worse. Soon she could barely turn her head. Driving became difficult. Even simple movements were painful. For months, she lived in constant discomfort.

Eventually, she used sick days – something she rarely did as a nurse at the state hospital. Stuck at home, she became a reluctant viewer of daytime TV. This was before remotes or streaming, so once she set the channel, it usually stayed there. One dreary winter morning, that habit changed her life.

She groaned when *The 700 Club* came on. "Religious fanaticism," she muttered. But she left it on, sipping her coffee. Near the end of the program, co-host Ben Kinchlow spoke about faith, quoting Matthew 17:20, "If you have faith as small as a mustard seed..." Then he invited viewers to place a hand on their TV as he prayed for healing.

Mom hesitated. Then she thought, *Surely I have that much faith.* She hobbled across the room, placed her hand on the screen, and prayed. Doubts came – she pushed them aside. And then it happened.

She felt warmth – like honey pouring down from her head through her neck and shoulders. She stood still, not wanting to break the moment. When she finally moved, the pain was gone. Completely. For the first time in months, she could turn her head freely.

Months later, she shared her testimony on *The 700 Club*. Friends, neighbors, and coworkers confirmed what they saw – not just in her body, but in her spirit. Once quick with sarcasm and self-pity, she became a voice of encouragement. She led women's groups. She started a church charity for the needy. She spent the rest of her life serving the poor, the broken, and the lonely.

I thought of her story recently while reading John 5:39–40 in *The Message* commentary Bible:

"You have your heads in your Bibles constantly because you think you'll find eternal life there. But you miss the forest for the trees. These Scriptures are all about me! And here I am, standing right before you, and you aren't willing to receive from me the life you say you want."

My mom wasn't a scholar. She wasn't even a regular churchgoer. She was just a hurting person who found a reason to hope – and then found the One who met that hope.

Maybe that's you today. Maybe your faith feels too small, too weak, too ordinary. Jesus says that's enough. Even a mustard seed of faith – when placed in the right hands – can move mountains.

And He is still saying, "Here I am. Come to me. Receive the life you say you want."

Growth

What part of your life feels stuck, broken, or hopeless? What would it look like to bring even mustard seed faith to Jesus in that place?

Grace

Even the smallest faith, when placed in Jesus' hands, can lead to life-changing miracles.

Week 37 —
MVP

"By this everyone will know that you are my disciples, if you love one another" (John 13:35).

Crack! With one powerful swing, Albert Pujols broke my heart – again. Bottom of the ninth. Bases loaded. Two outs. My team – the Cincinnati Reds – up by two. All we needed was one out. But instead of walking him, they pitched to Albert. Bad idea. The ball sailed over the fence for a grand slam. Reds lose. Game over.

Now, here's the strange part, even though I'm a die-hard Reds fan and the Cardinals are our archrivals, Albert Pujols is still one of my favorite players. Why? Because as great as he is on the field – a three-time MVP, a World Series champion, one of the most consistent hitters in history – baseball isn't the most important thing in his life.

In 2008, Albert received the Roberto Clemente Award. Clemente was one of my childhood heroes – not because I liked the Pirates (I didn't), but because he lived out his beliefs through service. Albert's done the same, using his platform to change lives off the field.

That's real MVP stuff.

Jesus put it this way:

"By this everyone will know that you are my disciples, if you love one another" (John 13:35).

Love isn't just warm feelings or nice words. It's action. Concern for others. The kind of action you see in Jesus' parable of the Good Samaritan (Luke 10:25–37). Remember? A man is beaten and left for dead. Two religious leaders walk past without lifting a finger. But a Samaritan – a guy who should've despised him – stops, treats his wounds, and pays for his care.

Jesus' command is simple, "Go and do likewise."

That raises the tough question, am I more like the Samaritan, or more like the guys who passed by? Honestly, it's easier to stay busy, keep my eyes down, and focus on my own stuff. But Jesus makes it clear, if I'm serious about following Him, my love should be visible.

Oswald Chambers once wrote, "Who of us would dare to stand before God and say, 'My God, judge me as I have judged others?'" Ouch. That's a reminder that when I see someone hurting, it's not my job to decide whether they deserve help – it's my job to love them.

Jesus also said, "The thief comes only to steal and kill and destroy; I have come that they may have life, and have it to the full" (John 10:10).

That's God's vision, a full, abundant life – not just for me, but for everyone. And often, the way He provides it is through us – His people choosing to love with action.

So maybe it's time to ask, am I on the field, or am I still warming the bench? Am I showing up for others in a way that proves God's love is real?

Because in God's kingdom, the MVPs aren't the ones with trophies, stats, or headlines. They're the ones who let His love show in action.

Growth

If love is measured by action, how's your game right now? Are you stepping up to the plate, or are you still sitting on the bench?

Grace

In God's kingdom, the true MVP is the one who shows His love in action.

Week 38 — *Screwed Up*

"But just as he who called you is holy, so be holy in all you do" (1 Peter 1:15).

I read that verse this morning and thought, *Yeah, right. Holy? Me? Not even close.*

Sure, I try. I love my family. I help when I can. I try to be kind. But holy? Half the time I can't even get through a prayer without messing it up. I'll be talking to God, and then suddenly a memory surfaces of someone who wronged me. Before I know it, I've gone from praying to plotting revenge. That's not holy – that's petty. And it happens more often than I care to admit.

Last night, sitting on the porch, I was hashing it out with God, confessing how often I still screw up. After all these years of knowing Him, why is sin still so easy? Why do I fall into the same selfish patterns? Why do I blow it when I know better?

And then my thoughts drifted to one of my kids – something selfish they'd done recently – and that familiar gut-punch landed, *I've failed as a parent.*

That's when an odd thought crossed my mind. In the quiet, I almost felt God whisper, *I know the feeling.*

Now, maybe that was just my imagination. But it made me wonder – does God ever feel like a failure when His kids mess up? Does He look down at our messes and think, *I haven't done enough?* I don't know. But here's what I do know, He cares deeply about what we do – not because He's keeping score, but because He knows where our choices lead. Pain. Consequences. Regret.

That's exactly how I feel with my kids. I don't want to control them with rules. I want them to live free – but in a way that doesn't destroy them. And when they make mistakes, I don't stop loving them. I want to help them grow. Isn't that exactly what God wants for us?

Paul put it bluntly:

"It is for freedom that Christ has set us free" (Galatians 5:1).

Freedom from the penalty of sin. Freedom from the hopeless treadmill of trying to keep every rule perfectly in order to be "good enough." Freedom from the lie that God is just waiting for us to fail again.

Holiness, then, isn't about being flawless. It's about living free – choosing, day by day, to let God's love shape our decisions instead of our anger, fear, or selfishness.

Peter said it like this:

"Therefore, prepare your minds for action; be self-controlled; set your hope fully on the grace to be given you when Jesus Christ is revealed. As obedient children, do not conform to the evil desires you had when you lived in ignorance. But just as he who called you is holy, so be holy in all you do; for it is written, 'Be holy, because I am holy'" (1 Peter 1:13–17).

That's not God demanding perfection – it's God inviting transformation. A new way to live.

And Paul summed it up in one line:

"The entire law is summed up in a single command, 'Love your neighbor as yourself'" (Galatians 5:14).

So yes, I'm screwed up. I mess up my prayers. I let my temper get the better of me. I carry regret longer than I should. But God hasn't called me to perfection – He's called me to freedom, to love, to holiness that looks less like spotless performance and more like daily surrender.

Holiness isn't about flawless track records – it's about leaning into grace. It's about choosing to get back up, choosing to trust God again, and choosing to love people – even the ones who make it hard.

That's something even screw-ups like me can do. And so can you.

Growth

When you hear the word holy, do you immediately think about your failures – or God's grace? What's one choice you can make today that reflects His love instead of your flaws?

Grace

Holiness isn't perfection – it's choosing daily to live in God's freedom and love, one imperfect day at a time.

Week 39 —
Whoa, Nellie!

Corrie Ten Boom once said, "If the devil can't make you sin, he'll make you busy."

Two friends meet in a store and exchange the usual greetings:

"How are you? It's been so long!"

"Good, good – just really busy."

"Me too. I saw your vacation pictures. Sorry I missed your grandpa's funeral… just so busy, you know."

Psychologist Carl Jung once observed, "Hurry is not of the devil; hurry is the devil."

That's where my sticky note comes in. Right on my desk, in plain view, are the words, "See people, not tasks." It's my personal "Whoa, Nellie!" A reminder to hit the brakes before I let busyness trample over what actually matters. Too often, I get so focused on what needs to be done that I overlook who is right in front of me. Relationships matter more than to-do lists… yet busyness has a way of blinding us to that truth.

Studies have shown that goldfish have an average attention span of nine seconds. Disturbingly, a Microsoft study suggests humans now average only eight seconds. How can that be? I believe it's because we're constantly flooded with things to look at, read, watch, and respond to – especially through our digital devices. We tell ourselves we're staying informed and connected, but at what cost?

Every day, people ignore those physically present in order to pay attention to those connected via social media or messaging apps. These conversations often consume our attention and energy – sometimes with people we barely know.

Modern convenience has made it possible to live almost entirely without personal interaction. We can shop, work, dine, worship, and even socialize without ever leaving home. It's possible to go days without a handshake, a hug, or even eye contact with another human being.

So what do we do? We have to be intentional – deliberately slowing down the frenetic pace of modern life and focusing on what really matters. The apostle Paul gave this counsel:

"If we live by the Spirit, let us also keep in step with the Spirit" (Galatians 5:25 ESV).

Paul didn't say, "Speed up." He said, "Keep in step." For many of us, that means slowing down enough to match His pace. In the same chapter, Paul describes what life in step with God produces:

"But the fruit of the Spirit is love, joy, peace, patience, kindness, goodness, faithfulness, gentleness, self-control" (Galatians 5:22–23 ESV).

If we're honest, we might see less of this fruit than we'd like. That's a sign we may be moving too fast to stay in step with Him.

Jesus invites us to a different rhythm:

"Come to me, all of you who are weary and carry heavy burdens, and I will give you rest… you will find rest for your souls" (Matthew 11:28–29 NLT).

Sometimes the way to catch up spiritually is to slow down – so we can walk at His pace, hear His voice, and notice the people He's placed in our path. Or as I like to remind myself, Whoa, Nellie!

Growth

Are you moving at a pace that allows you to stay in step with the Spirit? What is one way you can intentionally slow down this week to notice God's presence and people around you?

Grace

To keep in step with God, sometimes you have to slow down.

Week 40 — *That's Not My Thought*

"For our struggle is not against flesh and blood, but against the rulers, against the authorities, against the powers of this dark world and against the spiritual forces of evil in the heavenly realms" (Ephesians 6:12).

The first time I heard my mom yell, "That's not my thought, Mr. Devil!" I nearly fell out of my chair.

"What are you hollering about?" I asked.

"I'm not talking to you," she shot back. "I'm telling the devil he can keep his mean old thoughts. I'm not going to take hold of them."

That wouldn't be the last time I heard her say it either. My mom was known for her kindness and her steady faith, but she was also fierce when it came to guarding her mind. She believed every thought wasn't automatically hers to own. Some came straight from an enemy who would love nothing more than to plant lies and watch them grow.

And she was right. Jesus didn't mince words when describing our enemy:

"He was a murderer from the beginning... there is no truth in him... he is a liar and the father of lies" (John 8:44).

Again in John 10:10, Jesus said:

"The thief comes only to steal and kill and destroy; I have come that they may have life, and have it to the full."

Life is hard enough without sabotage from the enemy. Between bills, health scares, broken relationships, and daily frustrations, our minds already feel like crowded highways. Add in whispered lies – "You'll never change," "God's done with you," "Nobody cares" – and suddenly our thoughts become a battleground.

That's why Paul reminded us that we don't fight with ordinary weapons:

"The weapons of our warfare are not carnal, but mighty through God to the pulling down of strongholds; casting down imaginations, and every high thing that exalts itself against the knowledge of God, and bringing into captivity every thought to the obedience of Christ" (2 Corinthians 10:4–5 KJV).

That's serious language – "warfare," "strongholds," "casting down." Paul knew what we sometimes forget, if we don't control our thoughts, they'll control us.

And here's the kicker, not every thought that crosses your mind is yours. Just because it showed up doesn't mean it belongs to you. The enemy can't force you to sin, but he can sure plant a seed and hope you'll water it.

Jesus Himself modeled how to respond. When Peter, out of love, told Him to avoid the suffering of the cross, Jesus didn't just hear Peter's voice – He recognized the real source behind it:

"Get behind me, Satan! You are a stumbling block to me; you do not have in mind the things of God, but the things of men" (Matthew 16:23).

That's what my mom was doing when she called out, "That's not my thought, Mr. Devil!" She was refusing delivery. The package showed up at her doorstep, but she didn't sign for it. Instead, she replaced it with God's truth.

Peter gave us similar advice:

"Prepare your minds for action; be self-controlled; set your hope fully on the grace to be given you when Jesus Christ is revealed" (1 Peter 1:13).

And later:

"Be self-controlled and alert. Your enemy the devil prowls around like a roaring lion looking for someone to devour. Resist him, standing firm in the faith..." (1 Peter 5:8–9)

Did you catch the pattern? Prepare. Be alert. Resist. Replace.

So the next time a destructive thought tries to take root – shame, condemnation, fear, envy – don't just swallow it whole. Call it out. Push back. Say with confidence, "That's not my thought." Then grab hold of one that is, the truth of God's Word.

Like my mom showed me, you don't have to accept every thought that comes knocking. You get to choose who you let in.

Growth

What negative thought has been knocking on the door of your mind lately? How can you reject it and replace it with the truth of God's Word?

Grace

You can't stop thoughts from showing up, but you can choose which ones you live with.

Week 41 —
Pride Rock

"Do not let your hearts be troubled. Trust in God; trust also in me. In my Father's house are many rooms… I am going there to prepare a place for you" (John 14:1–3 NLT).

I once had a very intense, memorable dream.

Through the fog I saw myself walk slowly, almost solemnly, onto the pinnacle of a high cliff that looked a lot like Pride Rock from *The Lion King*. Far below, a crowd of people milled about, restless and waiting. Then someone noticed me. Fingers pointed upward. Suddenly the crowd went silent, expectant.

That "me" on the cliff was wearing a magnificent coat – heavy, patchworked together from animal skins, each square representing a good deed or sacrifice I'd made in life. I spun slowly, showing it off like a model. But inside, I was desperate – not just for the crowd to admire the coat, but to admire me. Hunger for their approval consumed me.

The longer I looked, the clearer it became, this "me" wasn't happy at all. He was terrified – terrified the people wouldn't think the coat was good enough, terrified God wouldn't think he was good enough. His whole identity was stitched together from scraps of self-righteousness and fear.

Then, across the desert plain, something bright appeared. A man in white was running toward the rising light on the horizon. His garment was seamless – no patches, no seams, no effort of his own. It reflected the blazing light ahead. And the closer he ran, the clearer his face became – eyes bright, laughter spilling out, joy radiating. To my shock, I realized, he was also me.

But unlike the coat-wearer, this man never glanced at the crowd. His eyes were locked on the light. His joy wasn't in himself, but in the One he was running toward. And then the voice thundered from that light:

"Behold my beloved Son, in whom I am well pleased."

I dropped to my knees in the dream, throwing off the heavy coat. My heart cried out, desperate to trade places – to know His love, His peace, His joy.

Then I woke up. Wracked with tears and wide awake, I knew what God was showing me, two possible futures.

One, I could try to earn His approval, patching together a coat of good works and false humility, standing on my pride and hoping it would impress Him or anyone else watching. But on the Day of Judgment, it would be nothing more than scraps of dead skin.

Or, I could accept the white garment only He provides. Washed in the blood of the Lamb. Seamless. Whole. Not something I stitched together, but something He gave me. In that future, I would run free – not bound by pride or performance, but alive in His grace, accepted as His beloved Son, with a place prepared for me in His house.

Isaiah 61:10 says,

"I delight greatly in the Lord… For he has clothed me with garments of salvation and arrayed me in a robe of righteousness."

The truth is simple but sobering, I can't make myself worthy. Neither can you. But Jesus can. He already has.

Growth

What "coat" have you been stitching together from your own effort or pride? What would it look like to throw it off and trust Jesus to clothe you in His righteousness?

Grace

Don't settle for patchwork pride. Throw off the heavy coat and put on the robe He offers – seamless, spotless, and enough.

Week 42 —
In Living Color

"There is a time for everything, and a season for every activity under the heavens… He has made everything beautiful in its time. He has also set eternity in the human heart; yet no one can fathom what God has done from beginning to end" (Eccl. 3:1, 11).

In my humble opinion, Ansel Adams was one of the greatest photographers to ever pick up a camera. The man could take a black-and-white image and make it sing. Along with Fred Archer, he even developed the Zone System – a way to control exposure and development so every shadow and highlight fell perfectly into place.

Back in college, when I was studying commercial photography, I tried everything to emulate him. After all, if you want to be the best, you learn from the best.

But here's the problem.

No matter how hard I studied his techniques – every step, every detail – my black-and-white prints came out… flat. Mediocre. People would compliment them, but I knew the truth. They didn't reflect what I actually saw or felt.

I kept at it for years, chasing greatness in monochrome. And year after year, I came up short.

Finally, after one more frustrating critique session, a professor gave me advice I didn't want to hear, "Some people just can't see in black and white. Maybe it's time to discover what you are gifted at."

It stung. It felt like failure. But deep down, I knew he might be right.

So I gave it one more push – and then I quit trying to be something I wasn't. I walked into a camera store and loaded up on the most vibrant color film I could find.

Almost instantly, something clicked.

Color unlocked something in me. My photography came alive. Professors noticed. Classmates noticed. I noticed. I saw the world differently – and it was beautiful.

That one shift eventually led to a studio job at one of Arizona's top photography firms. Later, when I started my own business, I called it *Vivid Graphics* – because vivid is how I see the world. Especially in the fall, still my favorite season.

There's nothing like fiery reds, golden yellows, and deep oranges of autumn to stir my soul. Living near the Blue Ridge Mountains just fuels the obsession.

In the fall, when I step outside, I don't see death or endings. I see a masterpiece. I see brushstrokes of God Himself – red here, a splash of gold there, a streak of silver catching the light. As if He's whispering, *"Fall isn't the end. It's a season of change, and the promise of new life."*

And that picture, my friends, is in living color.

Maybe you've been trying to live in black and white too. Trying to fit into someone else's frame, someone else's system, someone else's definition of what "success" or "holiness" or "purpose" looks like.

But God didn't make you to be a knockoff of someone else's art.

He wired you a certain way for a reason. To see the world differently. To carry a perspective others need. To reflect His beauty in a way that only you can.

Ecclesiastes says God makes *everything* beautiful in its time – and He's set eternity in the human heart. That includes yours. So stop fighting the way He made you. Lean into it. Live vivid.

Growth

What unique way do you see the world that you've been ignoring or downplaying? What would happen if you leaned into that perspective instead of fighting it?

Grace

You weren't meant to fit into someone else's frame. You were created to see – and live – in full color.

Week 43 —
The Greatest Mystery

In a recent interview, celebrated physicist Stephen Hawking – one of the most brilliant minds of our time – was asked what great mystery he most wanted to solve. His answer surprised me, "I want to know why the universe exists – why there is something rather than nothing."

Think about that for a moment. The man who studied black holes, wrote best-selling books, and mapped the cosmos with mathematics was still haunted by the most basic of human questions, *Why is there something instead of nothing?*

He also admitted that, given the vastness of space and the smallness of human life, the idea of a personal God seemed "most impossible."

But that's the thing about impossibilities – history is full of them being overturned. People once thought it was impossible to sail around the world without falling off the edge, to fly across oceans, to send a voice instantly to the other side of the planet, to put human footprints on the moon, or to run a mile in under four minutes. Today, those "impossibilities" are history lessons.

So is it really impossible to believe that the God who made the universe also cares deeply for you and me?

Here's where I land, if you're a parent, how many children would you need before you stopped caring what happened to one of them?

If you're an artist, could you ever feel indifferent about your favorite piece? If you've planted a garden, would you shrug if someone destroyed it? We, with our small and imperfect love, still care fiercely for what we create. Why would God be any different?

Maybe the real problem is that we sometimes blame God for things He never did. Jesus told us plainly who the real destroyer is:

"The thief comes only to steal and kill and destroy; I have come that they may have life, and have it to the full.

I am the good shepherd. The good shepherd lays down his life for the sheep" (John 10:10–11).

The heart of God is not to harm, but to rescue, to restore, and to lead us into a life full of meaning.

So why don't some people "see" or "hear" God? It might be like a broken radio receiver – His presence is everywhere, but without the right connection, you can't pick up the signal. The good news is, He offers to fix the receiver, free of charge. Through Jesus, the broken connection between us and God is restored:

"I will give you a new heart and put a new spirit in you" (Ezekiel 36:26).

But even after that repair, it's easy to drift back into old patterns. I think of it like my own recovery from a back injury years ago. A hang-gliding accident left me in constant pain. Regular adjustments from a good chiropractor helped me heal, but only because I kept going back. My body needed time to relearn a healthier alignment. Skip the visits, and I'd slip back into pain.

Walking with God works the same way. He is the Great Physician, but we have to keep coming back to Him every day. Paul put it this way:

"Don't become so well-adjusted to your culture that you fit into it without even thinking.

Instead, fix your attention on God. You'll be changed from the inside out" (Romans 12:2 MSG).

And Jesus invites us with these tender words:

"Are you tired? Worn out? Burned out on religion? Come to me. Get away with me and you'll recover your life. Walk with me and work with me – watch how I do it. Learn the unforced rhythms of grace. Keep company with me and you'll learn to live freely and lightly" (Matthew 11:28–30 MSG).

That's the greatest mystery to me – not just that the God who made the galaxies knows my name, but that He actually wants to walk with me every single day.

Growth

Are you living with a "broken receiver," struggling to connect with God? What's one way you can let Him realign your heart toward the joy of walking daily with Him?

Grace

The God who shaped the stars wants to walk with you – every day, every step.

Week 44 —
The Real World

In 1992, MTV launched a reality show called *The Real World*. It promised to reveal what happens when you throw strangers into a house together and roll the cameras. The irony? Everyone who's ever watched it knows there's nothing "real" about it. People perform for the cameras. Drama is magnified. A better title might have been *The Un-Real World*.

I thought about that show one morning as I sat in my office, staring at the brick walls that surrounded me. I ran my hand along the stone, feeling its weight and strength. In that moment, it struck me how much my "real world" had shifted in just a few short years.

Not long before, I didn't have an office at all. I was out of work, with no prospects and no direction. Two years before that, I thought I had my "dream job," and I wrapped my identity up in it. A year earlier still, I was in a job I hated, feeling stuck and hopeless. Up and down, high and low – circumstances shifting like sand.

But here's the truth I learned the hard way, for years, my confidence and sense of worth were rooted in my work. My paycheck. My performance. My position. I thought I was in control of my story. Until 2008, when the economy collapsed, and my sense of control crumbled right along with it. Suddenly, my house of cards was gone, and I was left holding… nothing.

That season forced me to wrestle with a question I'd been avoiding, *What is real?*

It reminded me of a Bible story – what happened the day after Jesus fed 5,000 people with just five loaves and two fish (John 6). That crowd had seen something miraculous, and their reaction was predictable. They wanted more. More bread. More miracles. More of what felt urgent. They even tried to make Jesus king on the spot.

But when they finally tracked Him down across the lake, Jesus didn't pat them on the back for their persistence. Instead, He said:

"You are looking for me, not because you saw miraculous signs but because you ate the loaves and had your fill. Do not work for food that spoils, but for food that endures to eternal life…" (John 6:26–27).

They wanted lunch. He offered life.

And many of them didn't understand. Some even walked away, saying, "This is a hard teaching" (John 6:60).

Jesus wasn't dismissing their physical needs – He had just met those needs the day before. But He wanted them to see that life's most urgent needs aren't physical. They're spiritual.

That hit me as I looked around my office – the desk, the lamp, the phone, the leather chair. Solid as they seemed, they were all temporary. One day, they'll be gone. One day, so will I. And what then? The eternal kingdom will outlast every possession, every paycheck, every position.

Not long ago, I sat with a man whose brother had died by suicide. His grief was heavy, the kind of grief that steals your breath. But beneath the weight of sorrow was something else – hope. His brother had known the Lord. That hope didn't erase the pain, but it gave him a foundation. It reminded me, in the middle of all this that feels "real," there's something deeper, stronger, eternal.

We're all like that crowd on the lakeshore. We appreciate the eternal, but we feel the pull of the immediate – bills, deadlines, groceries, a hundred daily worries. And the question keeps pressing in, *How do you let go of fear and really trust someone you can't see?*

Jesus gave us the answer in Matthew 6:

"Do not worry about your life... But seek first his kingdom and his righteousness, and all these things will be given to you as well." (vv. 25, 33)

That word *righteousness* simply means living in God's way – choosing to love Him and love others. Jesus wasn't saying ignore your needs. He was saying trust God with them, while you focus on what lasts.

So here's the challenge, if everything you owned disappeared tomorrow – your possessions, your pleasures, your position – what would remain? Would you be left empty? Or would you still be standing on something eternal?

That's the real question. And that's the real world.

Growth

Where have you been placing your identity and security – on things that spoil, or on what lasts forever?

Grace

The real world isn't the one you can touch – it's the one that lasts for eternity.

Stage 6

Love & Legacy

Week 45 —
River of Life

When I wrote this, I was in Nicaragua. The irony isn't lost on me – just a short time before, I had been researching and writing about rivers in western North Carolina. The New River, the Little River, the trout streams that crisscross our Blue Ridge Mountains. Home feels rich in water – lush and green, creeks overflowing, the land itself humming with life.

In Nicaragua, it's different. Dry. Thirsty. Even when it is technically the rainy season, storms are unpredictable. The heat presses down and lingers. Dust clings to everything. You miss the sight of rivers running strong.

I had been here the previous year, right before a pandemic that changed the world. Our small mission team had a plan – deliver supplies, encourage pastors, support communities – but plans shifted quickly. We got word about a village at the base of Nicaragua's largest volcano. Their well had collapsed. The creeks and arroyos had long since dried up. And now, the people had no water. None.

Picture it, mud huts patched with cardboard, plastic sheeting, and scraps of tin. No cars, only worn-out motorcycles and bicycles. Children barefoot in the dust. And now – no water to drink, no water to cook with, no water to wash or cool off in.

So we went. A five-mile journey took over an hour in a heavy truck loaded with water. Every rut, every rock, every bounce reminded us of what we carried – life itself, sloshing and threatening to spill. The day before, in a lighter vehicle, the drive had taken only fifteen minutes. But with a full truck, slow and steady was the only option.

When we finally rolled into the village, it was as if the whole place exhaled. People came running – women, children, and the few men not away in the cane fields – carrying whatever would hold water. Rusty buckets. Blackened pans. Old rain barrels. Even plastic bags. Anything.

The day before, we had brought toys and watermelons. The children laughed and played, their smiles wide. But this time? This was different. Their smiles carried something deeper than play. Their faces lit with relief, with gratitude, with hope. They had water.

I've served in soup kitchens. I've helped at community meals. I've supported local charities. But I had never seen such a pure moment – need and provision colliding so visibly, so powerfully, that gratitude seemed to hang in the air.

Take a mental trip with me. Imagine one of our dry spells back home – lawns brown, fields cracking, farmers anxious. Now stretch it to six months. No water in your faucets. No showers. No fresh drinking water. No laundry. No pools for kids to cool off in. Crops wither. Livestock weakens. Farmers sell what they can, but the harvest is pitiful. Then imagine it happens again the next year. And the year after that.

That's life in parts of Nicaragua. And still, the people stay. This is home. Their families have lived here for generations. They endure.

They wait. They hope.

And sometimes – praise God – hope is rewarded. Clouds gather. Thunder rolls. Rain falls in sheets. Rivers swell. The dry earth drinks deep, and the air fills with the sweet scent of a storm breaking the heat. Life flows again. And in that moment, there's only one response on every lip, "God is good."

"Si, si, si," I found myself saying with them. "Yes, God is good. And the rivers have begun to flow."

I went to Nicaragua thinking I was had something to give. But standing there with my hand on a hose, filling buckets that would empty again tomorrow, I realized something, we're all thirsty. Whether in North Carolina or Nicaragua, in plenty or in want, in green mountains or parched valleys – we are all dry and desperate for something only God can provide.

That's why Jesus stood and shouted to the crowds:

"Anyone who is thirsty may come to me! Anyone who believes in me may come and drink! For the Scriptures declare, 'Rivers of living water will flow from his heart'" (John 7:37–38 NLT).

The River of Life is not just for someday in heaven – it's for right now. It's His Spirit, His presence, His love flowing into the dry cracks of our souls, filling what has emptied, refreshing what has withered, bringing life again.

Pray with me for Nicaragua. Pray for the thirsty everywhere. And pray for yourself, too. Because when His provision meets our need, life flows – and gratitude overflows.

Growth

Where in your life are you feeling dry and empty? What would it look like to let the River of Life flow into that place?

Grace

When God's provision meets our need, life flows – and gratitude overflows.

Week 46 —
Tony the Tiger

I have a friend named Tony. Tony is my hero.

Now, before you picture cartoon stripes and a cereal box, let me explain. I call him "Tony the Tiger" not for the Frosted Flakes slogan, but for his strength – the kind that isn't about muscle or bravado, but about character.

Have you ever had a friend who, even though separated by thousands of miles, still checks in on you? A friend who won't let you disappear into the dark when life gets heavy? One who reminds you that you're loved and prayed for – not just with words, but with action? That's Tony. If he says, "I'll be praying for you," you can bet your last dollar he means it. He will take your name and your struggles before God as faithfully as if they were his own.

And here's what makes it remarkable, Tony himself carries a burden that would flatten most of us.

We went to high school together. These days, Tony is a Gulf War veteran living with a debilitating disease. Most days, he is too weak to sit up and eat or even type on his computer. Sometimes his wife or daughter helps him answer the hundreds of messages that come his way.

Why so many? Because Tony isn't just my hero – he's a hero to countless others. He encourages. He inspires. He prays. He listens. He checks in when you go quiet. Despite the battles raging in his own body, he spends his strength lifting others.

Why? Because Tony gets it.

Forrest Gump knew what "it" was too. My favorite scene in that movie is when Lieutenant Dan, now in a wheelchair, waits on the dock as Forrest motors by in his shrimp boat. Forrest doesn't hesitate – he jumps straight into the water, letting the boat crash behind him. Because when you have "it," you know, relationships matter more than anything else.

Tony understands that. But he also understands something bigger, you can't have that kind of strength on your own.

Tony's best friend is a lion – the Lion of the Tribe of Judah. Revelation 5:5 says:

"Then one of the elders said to me, 'Do not weep! See, the Lion of the tribe of Judah, the Root of David, has triumphed.'"

Tony draws his courage from Jesus. He would be the first to tell you so. He doesn't point to himself – he points to Christ. The verse that sums him up best is Philippians 4:13:

"I can do all things through Christ who strengthens me."

Now, let me be real for a moment. If I were in Tony's shoes – weak, limited, robbed of the life I thought I'd have – I can't honestly say I'd respond like him. I might be bitter. I might hide. I might shut the world out. But Tony? He leans in. He sees people. He loves people. And he does it with a joy that can only come from knowing the Lion of Judah walks beside him.

Here's the part Tony would probably squirm about, he doesn't want the spotlight. Writing this, I can already imagine him shaking his head and saying, "Don't talk about me, point them to Jesus." Fair enough. But sometimes the best way to see Jesus is through the flesh-and-blood faith of a friend who refuses to quit.

So let me ask you, do you think you've got "it" figured out? Are you trying to muscle through life on your own strength? Do you think sheer willpower is enough to face fear, disappointment, and loss?

Tony would tell you it isn't. He would point you to the source. He'd remind you of Jesus' words in Matthew 6:25–27:

"Therefore I tell you, do not worry about your life… Look at the birds of the air; they do not sow or reap or store away in barns, and yet your heavenly Father feeds them. Are you not much more valuable than they?"

That's the secret. That's the strength. That's the "it."

So when I call him Tony the Tiger, it's not because he's "grrrreat!" in the cereal-box sense. It's because he roars with a quiet, unshakable faith that points to something far greater than himself.

And that, my friend, is worth more than all the trophies in the world.

Growth

Do you have "it" – the kind of faith and love that keeps you strong for others, even in your own struggles? Where does your strength come from?

Grace

When your best friend is the Lion of Judah, you can face anything – and help others do the same.

Week 47 —
Kilroy Was Here

"Then those who feared the Lord talked with each other, and the Lord listened and heard. A scroll of remembrance was written in his presence concerning those who feared the Lord and honored his name…" (Malachi 3:16–18).

"You keep track of all my sorrows. You have collected all my tears in your bottle. You have recorded each one in your book… This I know, God is on my side" (Psalm 56:8–9 NLT)!

Brown County State Park, Indiana. Summer of 1975.

I was just a teenager, hanging out at a weathered old picnic table with three buddies. The wood was scarred with initials, declarations of love that promised to last "4ever," and plenty of doodles from bored campers who'd come before us. But one carving stood out from the rest.

Bold. Deep. Ornate.

It read, *"Kilroy was here."*

Kilroy had left his mark.

Something about it inspired us. We wanted to leave our own legacy, our own proof that we'd been there. So out came our trusty Swiss Army knives. Four boys went to work, scratching our names into that picnic table like it was the Rosetta Stone.

When we were done, we leaned back and admired our handiwork. We walked away proud.

That pride didn't last long.

The park rangers weren't impressed. Neither were our parents. Caught red-handed, we were handed sandpaper, stain, and varnish and told to clean up our mess. All our protests – "But the table was already covered in writing!" – fell flat. We'd been caught, and we were responsible.

So we scrubbed. And sanded. And stained. By the time we finished, that table probably looked better than the day it had been set in the park. All our marks, erased. Every scratch, gone.

Every mark except Kilroy's.

His engraving was too deep. It endured.

That day taught me something that stuck. What kind of mark am I leaving? Not on picnic tables or park benches, but on the people and places my life touches?

See, most of us spend our days trying to carve out a name for ourselves. Success. Recognition. Achievements. Some people even try rebellion, like carving initials where they don't belong, just to prove they existed.

But those marks don't last.

The Bible says something different about the kind of marks that do endure. Malachi tells us that God actually keeps a scroll of remembrance for those who honor His name. Psalm 56 says He collects our tears in a bottle, keeps track of our sorrows, and records each one in His book.

Think about that for a second.

The same God who created galaxies and spoke mountains into being also records your name, your prayers, your tears. While we're busy trying to scratch our initials into wood, He's engraving our lives into eternity.

That's the mark worth leaving.

Not the fading scratch of rebellion. Not the shallow etch of temporary fame. But a life marked by love, by faith, by obedience to a God who notices every detail. A life that points not to "I was here," but to "He was here."

So what about you? What kind of mark are you leaving? Are you carving something shallow that time will sand away – or something deep enough to outlast you?

Kilroy's carving endured on that picnic table. But even that table, eventually, will rot and fall apart. God's record book? That's forever.

Growth

What kind of mark are you leaving behind – and will it last?

Grace

The only legacy that truly endures is the one God remembers.

Week 48 — *No Greater Love*

"This is how we know what love is, Jesus Christ laid down his life for us. And we ought to lay down our lives for our brothers" (1 John 3:16).

"Greater love has no one than this, that he lay down his life for his friends" (John 15:13).

He rolled over, dazed, expecting the worst. The grenade had landed close – too close. He braced himself for the tearing pain, the searing heat, the end.

But it never came.

Confused, he checked himself – no wounds. Then he scanned for his buddies, each one like a brother he'd never had. They were all still there. No screams, no missing limbs. Somehow, against all odds, everyone seemed okay.

Trying to lighten the tension, he cracked a joke, "Must've been a dud."

But nobody laughed. Nobody moved.

Their faces told him something wasn't right. They weren't looking at him. They were looking *past* him.

Slowly, he turned.

And that's when he saw it – the broken, bloody body of a soldier, sprawled out behind him. The one who had thrown himself on the grenade. The one who had taken the blast that was meant for him.

With trembling hands, he reached down, brushing dirt and blood from the dog tags. When he read the name, his breath caught. It wasn't a stranger. It was a friend. *A brother in arms.* Someone who had decided that their lives were worth more than his own.

That's sacrifice. And that's love.

Sometimes people say, "There is no God," and I ache for them. Because it's in moments like this – stories of raw, unexplainable sacrifice – that we see what love really looks like. Love that saves others. Love that lays down everything. Love like Jesus.

And here's the truth, that's not just a battlefield story. That's the Gospel.

"This is how we know what love is, Jesus Christ laid down his life for us" (1 John 3:16).

Jesus didn't just say He loved us. He proved it with His own body, His own blood, His own life.

And here's the crazy part, He did it for you.

Yes, you – with your problems, your failures, your regrets, and your scars. He didn't wait for you to clean yourself up first. He didn't check if you deserved it. He just chose love.

"How great is the love the Father has lavished on us, that we should be called children of God! And that is what we are" (1 John 3:1)!

That's your identity now – not failure, not forgotten, not unworthy. Child of God.

But Jesus didn't stop with His sacrifice. He passed the mission on to us.

"Dear friends, since God so loved us, we also ought to love one another" (1 John 4:11).

That means we don't just talk about love. We live it. We sacrifice for it. We show it, even to the people who seem unlovable, unreachable, uninterested.

And let's be honest – that's hard. Really hard. On our own, it's impossible. But here's the secret, we don't love on our own strength.

"We know and rely on the love God has for us. God is love. Whoever lives in love lives in God, and God in him" (1 John 4:16).

We rely on Him. We draw from His well. And when we run out of love – which we will – He fills us again.

So here's the prayer:

"God, make me like Jesus."

Say it again.

"God, make me like Jesus."

That's a prayer He will answer, because it reflects His heart. He invites us to be living sacrifices – holy and pleasing to Him. Not out of guilt. Not out of obligation. But out of love. The kind of love that lays down its life.

Growth

Are you relying on your own strength to love others – or asking God to make you more like Jesus?

Grace

Love isn't proven in words – it's proven in sacrifice. Ask God to make you like Jesus, and He will.

If you think about it, being someone's child isn't a choice you get to make. None of us filled out an application or weighed our options before landing in the family we were born into. You didn't get a vote in who your mom or dad would be. You were handed into a family – messy or stable, loving or fractured, whole or broken.

For some of us, that family gave us roots of love and security. For others, those roots came tangled with pain, neglect, or questions we've carried for years. But whatever the story, one thing is always true, you are someone's child. That part was never up to you.

When it comes to God, though, the story flips. With the heavenly Father, you do get a choice. You get to decide whether to accept His free offer of adoption.

Paul put it this way in Galatians 4:

"But when the set time had fully come, God sent his Son, born of a woman, born under the law, to redeem those under the law, that we might receive adoption to sonship. Because you are his sons, God sent the Spirit of his Son into our hearts, the Spirit who calls out, 'Abba, Father'" (vv. 4–6).

That one little word – Abba – isn't formal. It's not "Most Honorable Father" or "Sir." It's tender. It's intimate. It's closer to "Daddy." It's what children say when they run full speed into their fathers' arms.

And here's the miracle, God doesn't just sign adoption papers and hand you a new last name. He sends His Spirit to live inside you, reshaping your heart from the inside out. That means Jesus' very character – His patience with the broken, His compassion for the hurting, His unshakable love in the face of betrayal – becomes the new DNA of your soul.

But let's be honest. For some of us, the word *father* doesn't bring comfort. Maybe your earthly dad was absent, angry, or unsafe. Maybe the very person who should have protected you caused the deepest wounds. If that's your story, please don't miss this, God is not the reflection of your earthly father – He is the perfection of what a father should be. Gentle. Patient. Protective. Present.

And unlike our earthly families, you don't have to earn your way in. You didn't earn your spot as someone's child when you were born – it was your first gift. And the same is true with your heavenly Father. His gift of adoption isn't based on your performance. You can't be "good enough" to deserve it. You simply receive it.

Jesus made that possible on the cross. He carried the weight of our sins – our failures, our selfishness, our pride – and opened the door wide. "Come in," He says. "You belong here."

The choice is yours. You can spend your life trying to prove yourself, trying to make your own coat of good deeds and hope it's enough. Or you can take the Father's outstretched hand, let Him whisper *Abba* over you, and step into a family that will never let you go.

Why not today? He's closer than your next breath, nearer than the ache in your chest.

Growth

Have you accepted God's offer of adoption, or are you still trying to earn your way into His family?

Grace

You can't choose your earthly, biological parents, but you can choose to become a child of the Living God.

Week 50 — *The Pink Pig*

"Look! I stand at the door and knock. If you hear my voice and open the door, I will come in, and we will share a meal together as friends" (Revelation 3:20 NLT).

"Don't worry about anything; instead, pray about everything. Tell God what you need, and thank him for all he has done. Then you will experience God's peace, which exceeds anything we can understand." (Philippians 4:6–7 NLT).

"I pray that God, the source of hope, will fill you completely with joy and peace because you trust in him." (Romans 15:13 NLT).

"The sink is leaking."

My wife's words trailed off as she walked out of the room, but the weight of them stayed behind. Another task. Another disruption. Another problem demanding attention – or else.

I sighed. The list was already long enough, owning a small business, serving in church, trying to be a decent husband, friend, and father. And just when I thought I was catching up, something else leaked – sometimes literally, sometimes figuratively.

It's not that I don't want to fix things. I do. But sometimes life feels like one long game of whack-a-mole, plug one leak, another springs up. Toss in the constant buzz of modern technology – the pings, dings, and notifications – and no wonder I feel like I'm drowning in distractions.

Then comes the holiday season. From late October through January, it's a tidal wave, gatherings, deadlines, decorations, shopping, wrapping, traveling, cooking, cleaning, expectations. And somewhere in all of that, I just want to breathe. To pause. To hear my own thoughts again.

Here's the truth I keep forgetting, peace doesn't come when the list is empty. Peace comes when I open the door to Christ. Revelation 3:20 reminds us that Jesus isn't barging in or shouting over the noise – He's gently knocking, waiting to be invited into the chaos.

The older I get, the more aware I am of my limits. The more willing I am to admit weakness, the more I realize what I actually need. Not fewer tasks. Not better time management. I need Him. Not just to get me through the season, but to sit with me in it. To give peace that doesn't depend on circumstances. Joy that outlasts the noise. Hope that leaks don't wash away.

I once heard a story about a man who kept having the same dream. He was driving on a narrow mountain road, and every night he'd pass a billboard with a giant pink pig. Just the pig – nothing else. Finally, frustrated, he prayed, "God, what's with the pig?" The answer came back in a question, "What did the sign say?"

The man hadn't noticed. The next night he looked again, and there it was in bold letters, *Don't Be Distracted*.

That's the sign I need too. Because life is full of leaks and lists and little things that demand my focus. But the still, small voice keeps calling, "Let Me in. Let Me restore you. Don't miss Me in the middle of it all."

The shepherds in Luke 2 weren't caught up in their checklists when the angel appeared. They were awake. Alert. Watching. Maybe that's why they didn't miss Him.

Growth

What distractions are keeping you from noticing Jesus knocking on your door today?

Grace

Don't let the leaks distract you from the Lord. Open the door – and let peace in.

Week 51 —
The Little Drummer Boy

"Jesus said, 'Let the little children come to me, and do not hinder them, for the kingdom of heaven belongs to such as these'" (Matthew 19:14).

I didn't grow up in a church-going family. We weren't against it – we just didn't make faith a priority. Our lives revolved around working hard, playing hard, and enjoying whatever we'd managed to build for ourselves. Spiritually, I guess you could say we stayed on the surface.

But then came Christmas. Once a year, like a spark in the dark, everything shifted. My parents hosted the family gathering – our house had the biggest living room and yard – and suddenly life felt full. Relatives packed in shoulder to shoulder, food and laughter spilled over, and Mama conducted the whole thing like a holiday maestro.

Mama loved yard sales, and she never showed up empty-handed. Every niece, nephew, cousin, and aunt had a gift waiting – wrapped in whatever she had on hand, newspaper, grocery bags, even leftover wallpaper scraps. They weren't expensive gifts, but they were thoughtful. And the joy wasn't in the price tag – it was in the giving. That annual rhythm of generosity planted something in me I didn't recognize until much later, it really is better to give than to receive.

Another tradition carried equal weight in my childhood, the Christmas TV specials. Our big walnut Zenith console would glow to life, and my sister and I would park ourselves on the floor to watch. My favorite – year after year – was *The Little Drummer Boy*.

Looking back, I think I know why. The boy in the story had nothing. No treasure, no family, no status. Just a battered drum and a song in his heart. But when he offered that simple gift to the Christ child, it was enough. More than enough. The baby Jesus smiled, and the boy's whole world changed.

I didn't understand the theology as a kid. But something in that story cut through me. Every time, I'd feel a lump in my throat and tears I couldn't explain. Why? Because even though I didn't yet know Jesus, He was already reaching for me – using a simple song to whisper truth, your gift, offered in love, is enough.

It still is. Maybe you feel like you don't have much to bring to God. You're not a preacher, not a missionary, not a scholar. But here's the secret, God's not looking for polish. He's looking for presence. He delights in the small, ordinary gifts we bring with love – an encouraging word, a listening ear, a meal dropped off for a neighbor, a steady hand at work.

The kingdom of heaven belongs to people who bring their "little drums." Because in the end, it's not the size of the gift that matters. It's the heart behind it.

Growth

What simple gift – act of service, moment of love, or creative expression – could you offer God this week?

Grace

Even the smallest offering, given from the heart, is enough to bring a smile to the face of the King.

Week 52 —
The Shepherd's Staff

"Even though I walk through the darkest valley, I will fear no evil, for you are with me; your rod and your staff, they comfort me" (Psalm 23:4).

A shepherd's staff doesn't look like much. Just a stick with a crook on the end. But out in the field, it was the original multi-tool. That staff guided, rescued, defended, and kept the shepherd steady when the ground was rough. A shepherd never set it down, because without it he and the flock were vulnerable.

That's the picture David paints in Psalm 23. God isn't a distant, soft-spoken cheerleader. He's a hands-on shepherd whose care is tough, practical, and personal – like that staff always within arm's reach.

I got a taste of this while riding in Nicaragua with a group of guys on what we called "moto missions." The "roads" were barely trails – steep rock faces, powdered gullies, blind corners – and we weaved through pigs, goats, kids, and cattle at full throttle. It was chaos on two wheels.

Honestly, I spent most of those rides praying, because one bad move could end it. And here's what I noticed, sometimes I felt a quiet nudge – almost like a soft hand pushing me to take one line instead of another. Every time I obeyed that whisper, I slipped through tough terrain unharmed, even while others crashed around me.

But other times, I thought I heard something louder, almost like a shout in my head, *"Turn here! Go there!"* Every single one of those "shouts" turned out wrong – straight into danger. God's whisper was steady. My own noise was reckless.

That's what the shepherd's staff is all about. It wasn't just a walking stick – it was a tool for survival. The curved end redirected wandering sheep. It pulled them out of ditches and thorns. It doubled as a weapon when predators attacked. It gave the shepherd balance when the ground was uneven. It kept things in order when sheep had to be separated. And it tested the ground before the shepherd stepped forward.

Every one of those uses points to how God works with us. He guides us when we start to drift. He rescues us when we're stuck. He defends us from what we don't even see coming. He steadies us when life feels shaky. He keeps order in our chaos. And He tests the ground ahead, clearing the way before we ever take the step.

God doesn't usually blast His will like a bullhorn. He nudges. He whispers. He steers. And when we follow that whisper, we find ourselves avoiding wrecks we never saw coming. Ignore it, and the loud voices of fear, pride, or self-confidence will send us straight into the ditch.

The shepherd's staff wasn't decorative – it was comforting because it worked. It meant the shepherd was close, not far off. It meant the sheep were never alone. That's the same comfort God gives, His presence is constant, His guidance is quiet but clear, and His grip is strong enough to pull us out when we're stuck.

Growth

This week, pay attention to the whisper. Don't confuse noise for God's voice. Slow down, listen, and let His nudge – not your own shouts – decide your next move.

Grace

The shepherd's staff reminds us that God doesn't guide from a distance. He's right there in the dust and danger with us – guiding, rescuing, protecting, and steadying. Trust His whisper. It's stronger, safer, and truer than the shouts in your head.

Last Call — *The Line in the Sand*

Here's the finish line – which is also the starting line. If you made it this far, you already know this wasn't about stacking up pages. It was about becoming. Week by week, God has been heating, hammering, and shaping. The grit of the stories hopefully reminded you to stand your ground – in Christ. Growth helped you think and change. Grace – through Jesus – met you when you couldn't muscle it. That's the work of real forging, not forgery.

Now keep it simple and keep showing up. Pick one small act of obedience each week – pray before you scroll, encourage one man by name, make the call you've been avoiding, show up at church even when you don't feel like it. Dog-ear the weeks that hit you. Start the cycle again next year. Hand this book to another guy and walk a few weeks with him. Iron sharpens iron, but only if it's close enough to strike.

My prayer is that the God who began a good work in you keeps shaping you into the likeness of His Son (2 Corinthians 3:18). Don't settle for looking the part. Step back into the fire, not the fakery. I'll see you at the forge.

www.ingramcontent.com/pod-product-compliance
Lightning Source LLC
Chambersburg PA
CBHW031130090426
42738CB00008B/1031